Slow Parenting Teens

*How to Create a Positive, Respectful and
Fun Relationship with Your Teenager*

Molly Wingate, M.A. and Marti Woodward, M.S.

Based on a cutting edge approach from teen therapist, Marti Woodward, and teacher, Molly Wingate, *Slow Parenting Teens* shifts the focus of parenting from teenagers' behavior to the relationship between parents and teens. Using commonsense psychology, the authors provide real-life examples of fast and slow parenting.

———◆ ◆ ◆———

"As a therapist, I am thrilled to find a parenting book that focuses on how parents make decisions instead of on teenagers' behavior. *Slow Parenting Teens* has a formula for creating long-lasting, positive change in the relationship between parents and their teenagers."

–Fred Dearborn, MA
Licensed Professional Counselor

"This cutting-edge approach has become central for me as the father of a new teen. With their spot-on knowledge and step-wise advice, Molly and Marti make me a better parent every time I practice slow parenting. Their five simple attitudes help me maintain the relationship I want with my son, and I share the ideas in *Slow Parenting Teens* with other fathers and mothers at every opportunity. I'm grateful for this book daily as I hang out with my son. Rock on!"

–Doug Gertner, Ph.D.
The Grateful Dad
www.thegratefuldad.org
Host of The Grateful Dad Radio Hour on
www.castlerockradio.com

"Simple, yet conceptual and practical, *Slow Parenting Teens* is a book designed to drive action. In that sense, it's a must-read for all parents and caregivers. This distillation of practical ideas, insights, and activities is designed to grow great teenagers and help parents nurture enjoyable relationships with their children."

–Amy Kelly, CEO,
Parent eSource.com & Socially Active.com

Table of Contents

Acknowledgments

(Bottom to top; left to right)
Hannah Arneson, Maggie Arneson,
Marti Woodward, Gavin Murphy,
Molly Wingate, Alex Arneson, Aidan Murphy

We would like to offer our deepest appreciation to our teenagers, in order of appearance: Gavin Murphy, Alex Arneson, Maggie Arneson, Aidan Murphy, and Hannah

Arneson. They have inspired us, laughed with us, encouraged us, corrected us, and been completely supportive as we wrote this book. We would also like to thank Brian Murphy, Molly's ever-patient husband, for his good parenting, his questions, and his fine humor. Ophelia Smith, Fred Dearborn, Vaughan McTernan, Jean Hannah, David Moore, Karen Rowan, Jeff Pike, and many others have cheered us on, shared their perspectives, tried out our ideas, and offered lots of love through the writing process. We also want to thank all the parents who took interest in Slow Parenting Teens, attended workshops, and read our blogs, newsletters, and Facebook page. Our work is enriched by their comments and challenges. Many of the examples in this book came from their real life experiences.

We feel heartfelt gratitude for Vern Turner who read every word of every draft. His reactions and edits grounded our ideas and presentation. We thank our agent, Krista Goering, for believing in *Slow Parenting Teens* and finding an outlet for it. And thanks also to Sammie and Dee Justesen and Nadene Carter of Norlights Press for pushing us to make this the best possible book.

Introduction

"Molly and Marti are bright lights with wonderful information and support for parents to grow their relationship with their teens! Thanks."
—John M., Denver

We were friends before either of us had children. We both had childhoods we wanted to improve upon for our own kids, and as it turns out, we had similar ideas about how to raise children. The most radical idea we ever had was to parent for a relationship with each child rather than parenting to manage each child's behavior. We see parenting as a way to build the relationships with our adolescents, not as a way to control them or try to mold them as people.

Who are we? We are Molly Wingate and Marti Woodward, the architects of *Slow Parenting Teens*. And we want to share with you what compelled us to write this book.

You see, we both cringe when we hear jokes about teenagers and how parents want to "bury them when they're 12 and dig them up when they're 22." It confuses us when other parents roll their eyes and congratulate us for surviving a house full of teenagers. We completely disagree with stereotyping adolescents as moody, self-centered, and a problem simply because of their developmental stage. And we absolutely do not subscribe to adolescence as something to simply "get through" until the teen becomes an adult. Mostly we are selfish and have no intention of waiting to have a relationship with our kids or putting those relationships on hold for years.

We both have close, open, and fun relationships with all of our kids. This isn't by accident; it's by design. Between us we cover a lot of parenting territory. Marti is the single mom of three adolescent girls, while Molly is married with an intact nuclear family and two boys. In fact, we were pregnant together with our eldest children over twenty years ago, and they have been close friends since kindergarten. Today, our relationships with our kids attract attention not only from other adults, but also from other teens. It seems both teenagers and their parents want to know the secret to actually enjoying each other and wanting to spend time together.

We believe the secret is Slow Parenting Teens.

We actually sat down to explore the idea of writing this book at the request of other parents. "What are you doing to help your kids open up to you?" is a common question, as is "I wish my kid shared with me the way yours does. What am I doing wrong? Please share what you're doing."

Many parents who've attended our workshops report immediate positive changes in relationships with their teenagers. Yet, for both of us, the greatest encouragement to write this book came directly from teenagers—and not just our own. When our children shared with their friends what we were up to, the other teenagers replied, "When will the book be out so I can give it to my parents?"

Your teenagers want a close relationship with you as much, or more, than you want the same thing with them. They lean into your acceptance, approval and attention. They pull away from your correction, judgment, and lectures.

Slow Parenting Teens is the parenting book recommended by teenagers. That alone was enough to convince us we needed to organize and share what we'd done privately for years with our own children and professionally with teens and their families for decades.

Can all parents achieve the same results? Does this work on all teens, or just those who are already open and communicative? Can you have a slow parenting relationship with your teen if the other parent doesn't share the same philosophy and style? What's the best age to start slow parenting, and is it too late by the time the kid is a teenager? What if one kid is an extrovert and another is an introvert? Does slow parenting work? We considered each of these questions while creating and exploring our model of slow parenting. The answer was the same for every question: It still works!

We also drew heavily from our professional experiences with teens. Both of us worked with adolescents for decades before raising our own. Molly has been involved with teenagers for over thirty years. After teaching high school, she moved to college teaching in 1979. For twenty-two years, Molly taught writing and directed writing centers at the college level. She taught composition and technical writing at Bucknell University in Pennsylvania and helped create a writing program and writing center there. She was a professional tutor for seven years. In 1987, Molly earned her M.A. in English and became the Writing Center Director at Colorado College. She continues tutoring teenagers who are graduating from high school and writing college application essays.

Marti has been working with teenagers since 1986 when she put herself through graduate school by working in a group home for juvenile delinquent boys. Since her graduation in 1988 with a Master's Degree in Counseling, she has worked in a locked hospital adolescent unit and a residential facility as an addiction specialist for addicted and dual-diagnosed teens. Marti specializes in family counseling and adolescent eating disorders, and has developed Family Programs for chronic runaway teens and their parents. She continues working with teens and their families as a life coach and a recovery coach for families struggling with addictions.

Between us, we've accrued over 40 years of personal parenting experience with five unique children, plus over five decades of professional work with adolescents and their families. We have worked with highly successful teens as well as dysfunctional teens. We have worked with cooperative parents and resistant parents. We've celebrated our own children's success and cried with them as they struggled with challenging life issues.

Our children are the guinea pigs for the Slow Parenting Teens concept, *and* our biggest cheerleaders. We consulted each of them before beginning this project, and they enthusiastically encouraged us to "write it down so other parents can learn to do this, too." They have helped us clarify concepts, and many of the examples in this book come from our own kids or stories we've heard of real situations for teenagers in the 21st century. Our children are our best and harshest critics, and here's what one of them wrote on our Facebook page, unsolicited, about *Slow Parenting Teens*.

"I really LOVE the way my mom parents. It has given us a relationship I wouldn't trade for anything. I want to tell her everything that goes on in my life because I know she will be truly interested and excited for me. I'm so close to my mom, and there is nothing I don't feel safe telling her. Even my friends say how much they wish they had a relationship with their parents like I do with my mom. This book will truly be the parenting book teenagers WANT their parents to read."
—Hannah Arneson,
14 years old (Marti's youngest)

Chapter One

Let Us Introduce You to Slow Parenting Teens

"A unique and cutting edge approach to parenting teens."
—Doug Gertner, *The Grateful Dad*

*H*ere's some good news: If the relationship you have with your teen isn't what you want, *you can change it.* You are the parent, and you've been designing and creating this relationship since the day your child showed up. However, you're the one who must make the first move—by changing yourself. And this truly is good news because it's much easier to change yourself than to mold another person. If you want a sustainable, respectful, and fun relationship with your teen, all you need is the willingness and motivation to change and persist in your efforts.

Our current culture says the teenage years are trouble; that teens are moody, unpredictable, unreliable, disrespectful, and unconcerned about anyone but themselves. This is hardwired into their physiology, and parents should expect contentious relationships. Struggles, fighting, and frustration are the only options.

We completely disagree. We believe the relationship between parents and teens can be terrific. We see the teenage years as ripe with opportunities for building fun, engaging, and close family relationships. Yes, teens *are* self-focused, but these are also the years when they begin looking outside themselves and their families. They are forming their own opinions and exploring options. As a parent, you can be part of the conversation as they learn to see the world differently and think hard about it—but only if you have a relationship with them.

Slow Parenting Teens shifts the focus of parenting from teenagers' behavior and appearance to the relationship between parents and teens. We want you to measure the effectiveness of your parenting not in terms of your teen's behavior and mood, but in terms of the type of relationship you have with him. Is the relationship positive, fun, open, accepting, and consistently curious? When you have a positive, open relationship, your teen comes to you when he has questions, is struggling with a choice, or discovers a new insight. When you have a closed, contentious relationship with your teen, she will not voluntarily come to you for anything. At best, she will tolerate you. At worst, she will hide, argue, lie, and shut down to avoid your consequences and your judgments. If you want a slow parenting relationship with your teen, then it's your job to change how you parent. We will show you how.

◆　◆　◆

Slow Parenting Teens was inspired by the slow food movement. Slow food encourages people to enjoy their food by being purposeful, mindful, and proactive about what they eat. Slow food urges us to eat local, sustainable foods and take time to enjoy meals. The slow food movement came about as a response to the fast food epidemic. Eating fast food is usually a habit, a reaction to situations, or the result of poor role models. It means pulling into the drive-thru lane because you don't have time to prepare a meal at home, you can't tolerate the kids' fussing and complaining, or because that's what your parents did. You manage the immediate problem, but you aren't providing the healthiest nutrition or acting as the best role model for your family. In essence, fast food is a reaction to a set of circumstances, not a thoughtful plan to provide nutrition for your family.

Slow food is all about planning ahead and looking at the bigger picture.

Like fast food, fast parenting is a reaction—this time to a teen's behavior or a family situation. Fast parents are sure they know what's best for their teen, based on their own life experience, and they feel remiss as parents if they aren't correcting their teen or voicing opinions and objections. Fast parenting focuses on immediate circumstances and the teen's behavior, in a reactive way. Fast parents have an answer to every question or situation, and that's probably how they were raised. This approach tends to be punitive, at least in the eyes of the teen. These parents rarely, if ever, admit their mistakes. They are good at rationalizing. Fast parents feel they must always have their act together; they don't tolerate having their decisions questioned. After all, if they listen to objections, their teen might view it as permission to go against them. Or the teen may discover a flaw in her parents' reasoning and use it against them.

Fast parenting is motivated by fear. Parents worry about how their teen's behavior will reflect on them, and they fear having their parental authority questioned. If something about the teen is unacceptable to the parent, then the fast parent wants it corrected—now. This is how they see their job as parents, and they couch it as guiding, teaching, and keeping their teen safe. Allowing a teen to make decisions is irresponsible parenting. Their job is to correct and direct their children.

Slow parenting challenges you, as a parent, to think differently about your role and consider how you and your child relate to each other. We ask you to look at the larger picture when making decisions. Slow food encourages us to be thoughtful about what we eat, how we cook, and how we enjoy our meals. This approach to eating emphasizes natural ingredients, traditional recipes, and taking time to enjoy a meal with others. Slow parenting encourages parents to be proactive about the relationship with their teen, to appreciate the uniqueness of each teen, and to create opportunities for talking and interacting.

Slow parenting is about your teenager's development, motivated by complete acceptance of each teen's personality. Parents and teens discuss, ask questions, experiment, and revise their ideas together. Slow parents arrange their schedules so they are regularly available. Slow parents are supportive, responsive, and focus on a long term relationship.

Fast parenting and slow parenting are two ends of a continuum; no parent is entirely one way or the other all the time. The same parent may be a faster parent when it comes to school work and a slower parent when it comes to their kid's appearance. This continuum leaves room for flexibility and creativity. Our goal is to help you move closer to slow parenting so you can achieve the relationship you want with your teen. If changing or improving how you and your teenager relate isn't your goal, then this may not be the parenting book for you. If you *do* want a better relationship with your son or daughter, then read on to see what's possible.

A slow parenting relationship looks like this: When your teen needs support, he readily asks for it. When she solves a problem herself, she comes to you to celebrate. He doesn't fear your judgment, so he uses you as a sounding board to talk things out. You and your teen can agree to disagree. You both easily apologize for mistakes. You and your teen laugh together often. You like your teen and truly enjoy her company. He wants you to meet his friends; you like them, and the friends like you. Your relationship is affectionate. Your teen feels free to express herself openly and honestly and is rarely disrespectful. You experience no drama around discipline; it is matter of fact, to the point, and clear for both of you. You choose to trust your teenagers, even knowing you often don't get the whole truth, and they trust you to not judge them. Slow parenting is a philosophy and an attitude.

Slow Parenting Teens encourages you to celebrate the unique people you get to raise, including *their* personality, *their* reality, and *their* context, while keeping an eye on the relationship you wish to have. Slow parenting is about creating and sustaining a positive, open relationship with teenagers; it is not about managing teenagers' behavior.

───◆ ◆ ◆───

In the next chapter, you'll answer questions about how you parent, and then plot your answers on a graph to determine your parenting score. You'll be able to see where you stand on the continuum between fast and slow parenting.

In Chapter Three, we introduce two ideas at the foundation of Slow Parenting Teens. First, we ask you to answer the question, "What are you afraid of?" Unacknowledged fears lead to fast parenting, and you will have difficulty moving toward *slow* if you don't uncover and address these sources of anxiety. Fears about your teen hinder a sustainable, enjoyable, and respectful family relationship. You subconsciously want your teen to change her behavior so you no longer feel worried and afraid. Teens intuitively pick up on this need to make them responsible for your emotional comfort, and they pull away and feel resentful. When you acknowledge your own fears and don't inadvertently make them your teenager's responsibility, you can start building a sustainable relationship.

The second big idea is this: we want you to rethink your primary job as a parent. Instead of policing your teen's behavior and moods, we want you to think of your job as creating a safe, nonjudgmental place for your teen, no matter what mood she's in. You want her to feel safe about sharing her opinions, and you want her to make choices without worrying about your judgment. When you focus on creating this place for your teen to be herself, you'll be well on your way to a slow parenting relationship.

The next five chapters of the book explain the five attitudes of *Slow Parenting Teens* which, when taken together, form the blueprint for a slow parenting relationship with the teens in your life. We devote a chapter to each attitude, contrasting fast and slow parenting as we go. After discussing the five attitudes, we address slow parenting and the setting of boundaries and punishments.

The following chapters discuss what to expect as you move toward slow parenting. You'll see how slow parenting plays out in complex family arrangements and in families with big problems. Finally we offer a chapter of resources for you to explore.

Let's start with a brief overview of the five attitudes for Slow Parenting Teens.

Attitude—#1 *Steward your teen*

Stewarding Your Teen forms the foundation for all the other attitudes. By stewarding, we mean paying close attention to who your teen is and how he or she changes from day to day. Know that your teenager is a work in progress. Parents who steward know their teen's disposition, allowing them to guide and nurture, not manage. To steward teenagers it's important to stay curious about them, pay attention to them, and make parenting decisions that consider who they are—especially since that may be different today than two days (or two hours) ago.

Attitude—#2 *Respect your teen's personality*

We use a broad definition of personality for this attitude, including such things as a teen's likes, dislikes, opinions, preferences, learning style, and whether he's introverted or extroverted. For a slow parenting relationship, we urge you to see and hear your teenager for who and what she is, not what she isn't—and definitely not what *you* want her to be.

When you respect her personality, you don't need to change her; you don't judge her, and you let her be different from you.

Attitude—#3 *Catch them doing it right.*

As a parent, you see your teen doing both what you want him to do and what you don't want him to do. You choose what to focus on. As you build a positive relationship with your adolescent, we ask you to point out what your teenager does right instead of what he could have done better or did wrong. With this attitude, you celebrate his choices rather than correct his behavior. As a result, your teen will start listening for what you have to say instead of tuning out the moment he hears your voice.

Attitude—#4 *Listening is effective.*

This attitude dovetails with the previous one. We want you to listen to, not lecture, your teenager. True listening means you want to hear and you're curious about your teen's story. This might be a synopsis of her day, an argument she had with a friend, or a new idea about what she wants to do with her life. We urge you to listen without judging, interrupting, taking over the conversation, or wanting the story to have a different outcome. When you truly listen, you develop the building blocks for a quality relationship.

Attitude—#5 *Parent every day.*

We suggest you devote part of *every* day to your relationship with your teenager. Your teen changes each day, and new challenges and celebrations arise. You will make a huge shift toward slow parenting when you're reliable and available. This attitude is necessary if you want to succeed with the other four slow parenting attitudes. You'll find it hard to steward, respect, listen, and praise if you aren't interacting.

◆ ◆ ◆

The following chapters discuss these attitudes in detail, including examples of how we use them. We point out the benefits of slow parenting and compare fast and slow parenting styles. We give you tips, hints, and homework to practice as you apply the five attitudes. Slow Parenting Teens challenges common parenting assumptions. We don't ask how parents can get teenagers to behave; we ask how you can establish a sustainable, mutually enjoyable relationship with the teenagers in your life.

Chapter Two

Are You a Fast or Slow Parent?

> *"Slow down, you move too fast."*
> —Simon and Garfunkel

*P*arenting is not all slow or fast. Even the most devoted slow parent has moments of fast parenting, and that's normal. You have your hot button issues and react strongly to them, often without much thought. These points of contention usually form around the things you fear most, causing you to act without thinking. Most fast parenting is based on *reacting*, which is why gaining self-awareness is so important. The more you know yourself, the less reactive your parenting choices will be.

This chapter will move you toward a stronger relationship with your teenager by helping you explore the continuum between fast and slow parenting. You'll see what issues touch your hot buttons, including sex, drugs, fighting, or talking back. If you spend time honestly looking at how you parent, you'll know where to focus your efforts as you make the shift to slow parenting.

EXERCISE

Please answer the questions below as honestly and quickly as you can. Pick the answer that best describes your family's experience or the answer that feels most natural to you.

Then, score yourself and see where you rate on the continuum between fast and slow parenting. These questions have no right or wrong answers. Your responses will give you a baseline so you can quickly move toward the relationship you want with your teenager.

1. Your son's teacher calls to tell you he's failing algebra. Your response:
    a. You discuss this news with your son and ask for an explanation.
    b. You ground your son so he can focus on studying.
    c. You ask him about his plan for handling this grade and how you can support him.
    d. You set up an appointment with the teacher, your son, and you so you can all come up with a plan.
    e. You check his grades online and create a plan for improving his grade.

2. Your 17-year-old daughter wants to travel with her friends for spring break.
    a. You say no, unless there's adult supervision.
    b. You tell her you'd love for her to go; you ask her what she thinks needs to be in place for this to happen.
    c. You say, "Sounds possible. Let's get together with the other parents and your friends."
    d. You say you'll consider it with a set of specific rules about the trip.
    e. You say, "No way, no way, no way."

3. Your 13-year-old wants to hang out with her friends after school at your house while no parents are around. You respond:

a. Okay, depending on who they are. Please don't eat all the snacks.

b. Can't you go to someone's house where an adult will be present?

c. Are you kidding? After what happened last time? No.

d. Yes, if you have all your homework and chores finished. Make sure their parents know I won't be here.

e. No. I'm not having all those kids in my house.

4. Your middle school daughter has a boisterous personality and is often in trouble at school.

a. You decide it's time to have your daughter tested for ADHD or ADD.

b. You make your daughter come to your meeting with the principal.

c. You tell your daughter you notice she's getting in trouble a lot, and ask her what she thinks is going on. Then you listen.

d. You sit and listen to your daughter's meeting with the principal and offer to support their plan.

e. You tell your daughter to straighten up, and you don't want to hear from the school again.

5. Your 14-year-old chooses to stay in his room after school every day.

a. You forbid him from isolating.

b. You bribe him to come out.

c. Why would you complain about a child staying out of your hair, especially when you're busy?

d. You establish the routine of having a conversation at some point in the evening so you can check in with him.

e. You poke your head in and ask if there's anything you can do for him.

6. Your daughter is mad when she comes home from school, and she snaps at you.
   a. You had a tough day too; you snap back and end up in an argument.
   b. You try to make her laugh to cajole her out of it.
   c. You let her know that taking her mood out on you is disrespectful.
   d. You ask if there's anything you can do her for and listen to what she has to say.
   e. You overlook the outburst, understanding it has nothing to do with you.

7. You came home to find your teenager has done most of the chores, but not all of them.
   a. You demand the chores get finished immediately and suspend all privileges for two days.
   b. You thank him for what he's done, then turn off the TV or take his cell phone until the rest are finished.
   c. You tell him how disappointed you are that the one thing you asked for isn't done.
   d. You lecture him about how often this happens and how sick of it you are, and that he needs to be a contributing member of the family.
   e. You walk in, notice the chores aren't finished and say, "Thank you for what you've done, and how are you going to handle this in a way that's satisfactory to us both?"

8. Your daughter is sure she needs to get new track shoes right now. You're sure it can wait until the weekend. Your daughter persists to the point of being rude.
   a. You tell her she's being disrespectful for questioning your judgment and refuse to discuss it until her attitude changes.
   b. You go to the store, but make sure she knows what an inconvenience it is.

    c. You suggest she calm down before you talk about it.

    d. You apologize for discounting her perspective, listen to her, and go to the store if you're convinced by her rationale.

    e. You say, "I need to calm down," and suggest you talk in half an hour when you can focus on her words.

9. You haven't seen your 18-year-old son for a few days because he's been going to volleyball practice early in the morning and each evening.

    a. You demand he skip practice to be home for dinner tonight so you can see him. You accept no excuses.

    b. You ask him if you can talk for 15 minutes before he goes to bed to get caught up.

    c. You arrange to meet him somewhere during a time when he's free.

    d. You let him know how this has affected you and your schedule and tell him he isn't keeping up his end of the work at the house, so he'd better not plan on going anywhere over the weekend.

    e. You let him know you want time with him and ask him to arrange it.

10. Your 16-year-old daughter tells you she's spending the night at Susie's house. You call Susie's mother in the evening and she has no idea what you're talking about. You call your daughter's cell phone, and she doesn't pick up.

    a. You leave a message that says, "No matter what, you are grounded and every ten minutes I don't hear from you is another week."

    b. You leave a message that says, "If I don't hear back from you in the next ten minutes, I'm calling the police."

    c. You leave a message that says, "I can't find you, and I'm worried. I need to know you're safe; call me as soon as you get this message."

    d. You leave a message that says you're going to start calling your daughter's friends and their parents, and then you do.

    e. You leave a message that says, "You have half an hour to get back to me, and then I'm going to start looking for you."

Scoring:

Use the grid below to score your results. The left column is the number of the question (1-10) and the top row is the letter corresponding to the answer. For each question, you may get 1 to 5 points. Circle the points you receive for each answer. For example, if your answer to Question 1 was "c", go to the row with the number 1 on the left and circle the 5 in the column under c. You received 5 points for your answer to Question 1. When you have circled a score for each question, add the scores together and plot the sum on the continuum below.

Q / A	a	b	c	d	e
1.	4	1	5	3	2
2.	2	5	4	3	1
3.	4	3	2	5	1
4.	2	3	5	4	1
5.	2	3	1	5	4
6.	1	3	2	5	4
7.	1	4	3	2	5
8.	1	2	3	5	4
9.	2	4	5	1	3
10.	2	1	5	3	4

10	20	30	40	50

Fast parent . . . . Slow Parent

Your score gives you an idea where your current parenting falls on the continuum between fast and slow parenting. There is no correct or perfect score. The only thing your score tells you is where you are today. Remember, this is information to help you improve your relationship with your teenager. Don't judge yourself if you aren't where you thought you'd be on the continuum.

10 – 20: Your parenting style is at the fastest end of the continuum. This means you tend to take control of parent-teen interactions and make unilateral decisions about how your teen will behave. You and your teen argue often and struggle to enjoy each other's company. Your teen shuts down, feels frustrated, and avoids your company.

20 – 30: Your parenting style is in the wide, middle band of the continuum, but tends toward fast. You and your teen struggle to get along, but sometimes things are good. You probably don't know many of her friends, and you may be surprised to find out later what she's been doing— good or bad. To maintain the status quo, she tells you what she thinks you want to hear. Many parents are comfortable with this spot on the continuum because it has the appearance of a "good" relationship when things are not contentious. Appearances are often deceiving.

30 – 40: Your parenting style tends toward slow parenting. You and your teen enjoy each other's company at least fifty percent of the time. You know some of his friends, and you both recover from arguments relatively quickly. You may need to be careful not to use guilt to get what you want, and don't be surprised when you discover your teen isn't always honest with you. He wants to keep the peace and have a decent relationship as much as you do. But neither of you share deeply or reveal too much.

40 – 50: Your parenting style is at the slowest end of the continuum. You and your teen genuinely enjoy each other and laugh often. Arguments are rare and you quickly recover from them. When she needs help, she comes to you. You notice her accomplishments and celebrate with her often. She doesn't feel judged, so she shares with you her struggles, thoughts, and choices. She wants your company and can be affectionate.

If your relationship isn't all you want it to be, this evaluation probably confirms that you're fast parenting more often than not. If you want to move toward slow parenting, keep reading. You'll learn about the changes you can make and how to actually arrive at them. But remember, Slow Parenting Teens measures the success of your parenting by the relationship you have with your kid. If you're looking for a parenting book that shows you how to manage your teen's behavior so he'll act a certain way, this isn't the book for you. If you want to achieve a better relationship with the teenagers in your life, then please read on.

Chapter Three

What Are You Afraid Of?

"If there is anything that we wish to change in the child, we should first examine it and see whether it is not something that could better be changed in ourselves."
—C.G. Jung

*Y*our job as a parent is to create a safe place where your teen can figure out for himself who he wants to be. If you want to raise a specific *type* of teen (high achieving academically, quiet, humble, generous, environmentally aware, or a star athlete), then slow parenting is not for you. But if you want a sustainable and positive relationship with a teenager who feels safe exploring who he is and will share his adventures, struggles, mistakes, and celebrations with you, then you want to be a slow parent.

The first step toward slow parenting comes in the form of a question: "When making parenting decisions, what am I afraid of?"

This is the most important question you can ask yourself. Parents typically make decisions without a great deal of reflection or even curiosity about their own motives.

We react to each new situation without considering our own fears and feelings.

If you want a slow parenting relationship with your teen, you have to slow down and be more deliberate about your parenting. Being deliberate means *knowing your own motivations and your own feelings.* Learn what you react to and why. What are your triggers and buttons? What makes you see red?

When you understand your own attitudes, you'll free yourself from the tendency to have knee jerk reactions. Instead, you will purposefully decide what you want to do.

Then parenting will become easier, and your relationship with your teen will be calmer. Asking "What am I afraid of?" should stop you in your tracks. This simple question will uncover your feelings and motivations for parenting decisions; in other words, your fears.

Once your kid hits the teenage years, she will activate your fears in a whole new way. Teens are harder to manage, and the consequences of their choices seem more life altering for both their lives and yours. So it's easy to fall into thinking, "If my teen would just _____, then I would feel better." You fill in the blank: "If my teen would just study harder, stop lying, go to bed on time, not talk back to me, be respectful, clean her room, come home on time, not have sex, not drink, go to church ... then I wouldn't have to worry and I'd feel better. And isn't it my job to keep my teenager in line and safe so he'll be a responsible person?"

For most parents, focusing on a teen's behavior, choices, and mood is easier than dealing with your own fears and insecurities. The natural tendency to avoid your own emotional distress is what motivates you to fast parent—and it happens so automatically that you don't notice. As a result, your parenting decisions are driven by subconscious fears and insecurities instead of your desire to build a sustainable relationship with your teenager. To slow parent your teen, you must focus on recognizing and managing your own feelings and fears, NOT managing your teen's behavior. This may be the hardest concept in the entire book, and it's also the most critical.

To discover your feelings, you need to acknowledge two kinds of fear: fear for yourself and fear for your teen. You're familiar with the anxiety you feel for your children: "Wear your helmet! Fasten your seat belt! Call home!" You may not recognize the fact that you're afraid of dealing with a new, negative situation: a child who's injured or in trouble. You believe your feelings are based on a noble concern for your teenager's well-being, but a deeper exploration can show you more. You also have selfish fears that motivate your actions and reactions as a parent.

You hide your selfish fears behind honest concerns for your teen. For example, you might say, "If you don't graduate from high school, you won't amount to anything." "If you get pregnant, your life will be ruined." "If you don't study for the test, you'll fail." "If you go to a party where there's drinking, you'll get in trouble." "You won't be taken seriously at a job interview if you look like that."

A telltale sign that you haven't acknowledged selfish fears is when you begin your objections with the pronoun "you." Your real fear is about how the teen's behavior will affect you and how helpless you feel when he or she makes choices that have consequences for you.

So how do you uncover your own fears? First, recognize the fact that you're probably not in touch with your selfish feelings. No problem, because we all have those issues. If you struggle to answer the question, "What am I afraid of?" or if your answer comes in terms of your teen, "I'm afraid she won't get into college," you haven't recognized the hidden fears that direct your parenting. To begin, identify your fears by listening to how you talk to and about your teen.

◆ When you talk to your teen, do you use the pronoun "you" most of the time? This indicates your teen's behavior (and correcting it) is the focus of your comments and she's probably doing something that scares you. Think about what provoked your comment. What selfish fear of yours is hiding beneath your words?

♦ When you talk to another adult about a parenting situation, do you only mention your teen's mistakes, misdeeds, and problems? Again, you're focusing on your teen's behavior, not your own fears. What are your underlying selfish feelings and fears?

♦ Do you find yourself needing to tell the story of your teen's behavior to someone else so you can explain or justify *your* reaction? Again, something in this situation scares you to the point that you have to rationalize your fast parenting. To slow parent, you need to understand your selfish fears for your teenager.

Second, make a list of what you're afraid of *for your teen*. For example,

He won't have any friends.
She will get a bad reputation.
He will fail the test.
She won't get into college.
She will get pregnant.
He will get someone else pregnant.
She will get a speeding ticket.
He will be hurt or injured.

This list is important because it brings you a step closer to what lies beneath your fears for your teenager. Your selfish fears are what *really* motivate your parenting.

Now make another list. What are you afraid of for yourself if your teenager doesn't follow your rules? This is the bravest thing we will ask you to do. Rather than rationalizing your fears, we're asking you to dig them out and name them. Look at the list of your fears for your teen, and write down how that situation will affect *you*. Ask yourself, "So what happens *for me* if he gets a speeding ticket?" "What happens *for me* if she gets injured or hurt?" This exercise is more challenging, but you'll gain a list of your true parenting motivators: your subconscious, selfish fears.

I will have to pay the ticket.

I will have to take time off from work.

I will be embarrassed by my teen's choices and behavior.

I will be judged a bad parent.

I will have to start driving him around again.

I will have to deal with her mood.

I will have to referee sibling fights.

It will cost me time, money, and reputation.

I will have to clean up his mess, and I will resent him.

The items on this list are not bad; in fact, they're typical. They may not be noble or pretty, but all parents feel this way from time to time. However, recognizing and being honest about this list will change everything. As you take responsibility for your own selfish fears, you'll open the door to a different relationship with your teen—one in which you no longer inject your selfish fears into your family dynamics. That is the secret to slow parenting—don't project your fears onto your teen.

Whether you know it or not, when you don't manage your own fears, you're expecting your teen to do it for you. This is projection. Your teen needs to behave in a certain way so you won't be afraid. When you don't own your own these fears, you make your teenager responsible for your emotional stability. This subconscious projection happens so quickly and without your awareness, that it feels natural. And it's much more comfortable than dealing with your own fears.

Picture yourself in a relationship with someone who issues dire warnings every time you drive your car: "Wear your seatbelt, check your mirrors, fill the gas tank, watch out for other drivers, and don't speed." You're a good driver, but your significant other makes driving seem like a perilous undertaking. At first you may be flattered by his concern, but after a while it gets annoying because you see that he's projecting his anxiety onto you. His worry undermines your confidence.

We want you to be conscious your own selfish fears so you can stop disguising them as noble concerns for your teen. Your teen resents your projections.

How can you tell when you're projecting? Examine how your teen interacts with you. A teen who feels responsible will react to her parent's fears in one of two ways: she will try to hide anything she does that causes her parent to have uncomfortable feelings, or she'll adjust her behavior according to what she thinks her parent wants in an attempt to help her parent feel less afraid.

In the first case, the teenager becomes cautious, edits everything he says, and is defensive; he hides, lies, avoids, diverts, or shuts downs in an attempt to keep his parent from being upset or angry. In the second case, the teenager who tries to protect her parent's feelings bends over backwards to keep her parent happy, rarely takes any risks, has difficulty making her own decisions, can be a perfectionist, and lives in fear of her parent's disappointment or distress. A teen can also switch between being defensive and accommodating. The flip-flop teen ends up feeling frustrated because he can't sustain either stance and can't win, since his parent is upset or uncomfortable, no matter what. Whichever way the teen goes, he is not in a sustainable relationship with a parent. By subconsciously accommodating his parent's fears, the teen accepts responsibility for them, and he resents it.

This projecting and accommodating dynamic happens beneath the surface of your relationship. If you want to see it, you need to look. If your teen resents your fears, you will see a moody, quick-to-anger, easily fed up, shut down, noncommunicative, rude teen who acts out to get the attention back on him. The accommodating teen will be unable to make a decision for herself; is stressed out about academic, social, and athletic performance; rarely breaks any rules; is nervous; has a deep need to understand what people want from her; and shares only surface information with her parents. She works hard to have an emotionally stable climate at all times, and she deeply fears someone will be upset with her—especially a parent. She will either reject her parent or work harder to maintain the equilibrium, but she will rarely, if ever, share her feelings. When you discover and own your fears as the parent, you make it easier for your teen to approach you when she wants to celebrate and when she needs support.

To own and acknowledge your fears, we suggest saying them out loud to your teens. You will still parent from these fears, but when you own them you no longer tell your teens, "My rules are for your own good." You both understand that many of your rules are simply to take care of your selfish fears, and that's okay. You still parent, you still make rules, but no one pretends they're just for the teen's wellbeing. For example, you can say to your teenager, "You have a curfew because I want to sleep," instead of, "You have to be in by eleven because you need to be at work tomorrow morning."

When you handle your own feelings and your fears, your teenager will feel the difference, consciously or not. First, they don't have to accommodate your feelings and reactions, and thus they have permission to focus on themselves and their own feelings and choices. Second, they don't have to "buy into" the idea that your parenting is for their own good. When you're honest about your selfish fears, your teen is more likely to respect your rules, whether she agrees with them or not.

Think about it: how would it feel for your teen to have a relationship with you where she can start a conversation knowing she won't be corrected, blamed, or judged, and her experiences and perceptions will be validated? He will have the safety to explore, contradict himself, feel sorry for himself, be ashamed of himself, and come full circle to find his own solutions. This is your primary job as a slow parent: to create the one safe place for your teen to be authentically and utterly himself—with all his compassion, self-centeredness, moods, arrogance, humility, self-righteousness, and other contradictions basic to the human condition that are often magnified in adolescence.

How do you create this safe emotional place for your teen? We'll say it again: You start by owning your own fears. Once you do so, you become a role model and create a safe place for your teen to bring his fears, concerns, and shame. This doesn't happen overnight, and you won't do it perfectly. At first, she won't trust you because her experience has been that she must address your fears first. Teens intuitively know: behave well = parents happy; behave badly = parents unhappy. You have to persist in this new commitment to make your selfish fears your business, and not your teen's responsibility. With time, she will trust you not to put your fears on her.

Here's how owning your selfish fears with your teen looks in practice. Your teenager asks to go to a party on the weekend.

You say, "No."

Your teen asks, "Why?"

You say, "I'm still freaked out about the last party you went to and got drunk. I'm not ready to say yes."

And your teen says, "But it isn't fair that I can't go because you're freaked out."

You reply, "You're right. It's not fair, but I still say no because I'm not ready."

This exchange may seem like you aren't holding your teen accountable for her behavior. You could be missing a great opportunity to point out what she did wrong and teach her about consequences. Yes, it could be, but that isn't how to build a trusting relationship. Besides, she already knows what she did wrong, and she *is* experiencing the consequences. Instead, be a role model for how to handle your own fears and decisions by explaining them to her or by turning to another adult to talk about them.

———◆ ◆ ◆———

Here's another way to think about the power of owning your fears instead of projecting them onto your children: Most people behave as if their feelings are a response to someone else's behavior. Let's follow that logic. If you believe your feelings are solely a reaction to outside stimuli, then each time you have a feeling you don't like, you blame someone else. You try to manage the other person rather than address your own feelings. This is especially dangerous with teenagers because they're sensitive to being held responsible for adults' feelings and fears. They have plenty of issues of their own; they don't need to pile on their parents' issues. As we said earlier, they become resentful and pull away, or they try desperately to accommodate your expectations. You will have success building a slow parenting relationship when you own your selfish fears rather than trying to manage your teen's behavior so you can avoid that fear.

This doesn't mean you don't parent; you still set limits and guide choices. The difference is that you don't blame the rules on your teen, and you don't spend time trying to get your teen to agree with the rules or limits. You simply own that the limits and rules are for your comfort, not the teen's wellbeing.

To slow parent, you must own your selfish fears, set the guidelines, and dole out consequences without framing your parenting in terms of what's best for your teen. Your job is to create a safe place, and the only way to consistently create that space is by owning your fears. That's why, "What am I afraid of?" is the most important question in this book. Your willingness to repeatedly ask and answer that question will determine how relaxed, easy, and fun your relationship will be with your teen. If the relationship you have with your teen is tense and stressful, it's because you put your fears into it and onto your teen. If you want to change your relationship, you need to own your fears. Owning your fears and creating an emotionally safe place for your teen will set the backdrop for the five attitudes of slow parenting. With the five attitudes, you will build a sustainable, respectful, and dynamic relationship. You'll learn to consistently interact with your teen in a way that doesn't make him responsible for your selfish fears.

EXERCISE

Distinguishing Between Noble and Selfish Fears

1. Go back and review all the exercises in this chapter. See if you can add to the list of your fears for your teen and fears for yourself. Notice where you struggle. Most of us have difficulty putting our selfish fears into words.

2. Start a journal and write every day for two weeks. Write about your fears for your teen and for you. This will help build the habit of thinking and noticing your fear before you react and parent on autopilot.

3. During those first two weeks when you set limits or discipline your teenager, practice telling him what you're afraid of, both for him and for yourself. Notice how he responds when you share your fears for him. Now notice how he reacts when you share your fears for yourself.

4. Talk with another adult about your fear, especially your selfish fears. Say them aloud and listen to the other parent affirm that she has fears as well.

Chapter Four

Attitude One
-Steward Your Teen

"Know what's weird? Day by day nothing seems to change,
but pretty soon ... everything's different."
—Calvin and Hobbes

*M*ost parents believe their primary task is to keep their children safe. We think that particular belief is an example of fast parenting—and a set-up for failure and damage to your relationship. Instead, we encourage you to consider our first Slow Parenting Teens attitude: Steward Your Teens.

Of course you fear for your children's wellbeing and want them safe. You never want to hear that your child has come to harm. However, when you make safety the primary focus of parenting, you discount your teens' judgment. They will resent your lack of confidence in them. While you hope things you say and do will keep your teens out of trouble, in reality they will be making their own decisions. When safety is the focus, fear for your teen is masking your selfish fears. If you allow this masking to occur, you try to manage how your teen behaves, and you are fast parenting. You react strongly and swiftly to any perceived threat to your teenager and unilaterally decide what should happen. Your fear will trump your teen's judgment.

These unilateral decisions damage the relationship between you and your teen. Sometimes he simply does as you say because it's easier or because he fears the consequences. When he concedes, the relationship between you becomes fertile ground for poisonous resentment or depressive passivity. He won't bother sharing his perspective because it won't be considered. He'll just go behind your back and hide the behavior as best as he can. This passivity is a sure sign that your relationship is suffering, even if you aren't battling every day. Battling or passivity are not okay, and neither supports a fun, relaxed relationship.

Believing you can parent your teen so he or she will remain safe is a dangerous mindset for you. With this viewpoint, you'll blame yourself for choices your teen makes or accidents that occur. Poor parenting didn't cause your daughter to burn her hand at work. Poor parenting won't cause your son to have a blow up with his coach. You cannot guarantee your teen's safety—physical or emotional. You may feel better if you think so, but that's a mirage.

Fast parenting for safety is a dangerous set-up for teens as well. They're blamed for accidents, and they get no credit for good judgment. Your daughter decided to refuse a ride from a friend who'd been drinking, but not just because you warned her against riding with a drunk driver. She used discernment. She made an appropriate choice, but she was late getting home and got a ride with someone you didn't know. If you're fast parenting, you focus on the fact that she was late, she didn't call home for help, and how she got in that situation in the first place. Your daughter gets no opportunity to share how and why she made her decision. She gets no credit or celebration; she only gets in trouble. Next time, she might not bother to tell you anything. Obviously, your relationship will suffer.

Slow parenting asks parents to focus on stewardship, not safety. Slow parenting holds that teens learn discernment and judgment with their parents' support and that such stewardship results in a positive, relaxed relationship. Slow parenting does not advocate ignoring safety concerns. We aren't talking about leaving loaded guns about the house or allowing kids to drive without a license. Nor are we saying you shouldn't call the parents of the teen who's hosting a party on Friday night to see if they'll be home. We aren't talking about abandoning *your* judgment. We're saying that life will happen to you and to your teen, whether you use fast or slow parenting. But fast parenting doesn't create a sustainable relationship with your teen, while slow parenting does.

To steward their teenager, slow parents adjust to their teen's developmental stages and include him in decision making. The steward of a forest quietly observes, notices what natural processes are going on, and monitors changes. A steward supports the land by thinning or planting after considering what will perpetuate the health of the forest. To make these choices, the steward must know the forest well and pay attention. We suggest a similar attitude for stewarding your teen. Know and observe her, ask questions, look to the future, and include her in conversations about her growth and desires. With this information, you can make positive choices about where to put your parenting energy. Through those positive choices, you build a sustainable relationship with your teen.

In practice, stewardship is the foundation for slow parenting, and we will talk about the forms it takes as we go through the book. Stewardship requires time, attention, and curiosity. Stewardship leads to an attitude of parental humility. You will learn that you're sometimes wrong about what's best for your teen. You learn that your teen is often correct about what he needs. We can spend a lot of time talking about safety, but keeping teens completely safe is impossible. You would do better to put energy into stewarding your teen as he learns to use his own discernment and judgment. In the end, you'll build a sustainable, relaxed, open, and fun relationship.

Stewardship sounds like a lot of work—and it can be. But think cost benefit analysis. Where will your effort have the most impact? Safety experts tell us we can't guarantee safety, but we can improve the odds of a safe outcome. We think you can improve the odds of a safe outcome *and* have a relationship. When you cultivate a slow parenting relationship with your teen, she will seek you out when she has a safety issue, and that will increase the odds of a good outcome for you both. Stewardship is the upfront investment for a long term, positive relationship.

Stewarding teens not only pays off in terms of energy but also in relationship quality. Teens feel cared for, but not controlled, and they're paid attention to, not judged. Teenagers gain self-confidence and learn to trust their independent judgment. Stewardship allows them to develop judgment and discernment with your support. Your teens are more likely to turn to you for support when you foster a positive relationship that accommodates their growth and development. So encourage them to test their wings while you're on hand.

With stewardship, you'll build a solid ground for the complete process of Slow Parenting Teens. We want you to have an unusually high level of curiosity about who your teen is and who he's becoming. We want you to know him, not correct him. To steward, you must pay close attention to him, marvel at him, enjoy him, seek out opportunities to be with him, and stay consistently interested in this ever-changing young person and his world.

Sharing living quarters with your teen isn't enough to truly know her world; you must stretch into hers. Becoming part of that world lets you know the context of her decisions and how she weighs risk. Most, if not all teens, have a method to their seeming madness. Your job as a parent is to learn how they make decisions so you can understand their vision and blind spots. With that knowledge, you can influence your teen by providing informed and expanded perspectives. But stewarding doesn't guarantee a teen will follow your advice. Your teen will ask for your opinion when she feels respected and free to make her own decisions. Just as the steward of a forest learns to work with nature's processes, parents who steward learn to work with their teen's natural development. Stewarding requires being curious about your teen's meandering without pushing her onto a specific path.

A real situation can help illustrate how fast and slow parenting differ with regard to stewarding. The first scenario concerns driving—that great rite of passage for a teen. A 16-year-old daughter walks out the door with car keys on the first Friday night after getting her license. She's smiling and happy. If you're fast parenting, you might have a conversation like the one below.

Mom: Where exactly are you going?

Sarah: I'm going to Jane's house.

Mom: Be home before dark; you don't have enough driving experience. Call me when you get there so I know you're safe.

Sarah: Okay, Mom.

Mom: Now remember, no texting, no phone calls, no one else in the car with you. No loud music, and fasten your seat belt. Are you going on the highway?"

Sarah: No, I'm driving on back streets.

Mom: Good, I'm just worried about you. You are not ready for the highway yet.

Sarah: Bye, Mom.

If you're slow parenting, the conversation might go like this:
> Mom: I'm so happy for you! This is cool. Off you go in a
> car by yourself for the first time.
> Sarah: Mom, you're such a dork! I'm just going to Jane's
> house.
> Mom: When do you think you'll be back?
> Sarah: In an hour or so.
> Mom: Have fun.
> Sarah: Thanks, Mom.

The big difference between these conversations is their focus. The fast parent focuses on her noble fears about Sarah's safety. The slow parent focuses on celebrating this rite of passage. After Sarah drives away, the slow parent may turn to another adult and address her selfish fears, "I hope she's safe! I hope she doesn't wreck the car, or get a ticket I have to pay. This is scary for me!" When slow parenting, you express your selfish fears to another adult, not the teenager.

Teen parties are another situation that brings up safety issues for parents. The fast parenting conversation goes like this:
> Hannah: I'd like to go to Anna's party on Saturday night.
> Dad: I don't know. Will her parents be there?
> Hannah: I'm sure they will.
> Dad: You know if there's any alcohol, you can't go. Will
> there be drinking?
> Hannah: No, Dad, not with her parents there.
> Dad: What time will the party end?
> Hannah: Actually, I'd like to spend the night.
> Dad: No. I want you home by eleven.
> Hannah: Dad, all the girls will be spending the night.
> Dad: There will be *boys* at this party?
> Hannah: Maybe, probably, I don't know.
> Dad: You're lying to me again, aren't you? I want to talk
> to Anna's parents.

Hannah: I hate this. You never trust me. You treat me like
    I'm a baby!
Hannah slams out of the room.

The slow parenting conversation would go like this:
Hannah: Hey Dad, Anna's having a party this Saturday.
    Can I go?
Dad: Most likely. Tell me about it.
Hannah: Well, the girls are spending the night and the
    guys are supposed to leave by midnight. Her
    parents are going to dinner but will be back later.
    We're probably going to eat pizza and get a movie.
Dad: Will there be drinking?
Hannah: Dad, it's a high school party.
Dad: Ok, so will you be drinking?
Hannah: I probably will have a beer, but I won't drive or
    leave the house. And Lucy is going, so you know
    I won't go overboard.
Dad: I, of course, would prefer you not drink at all, but
    it sounds like you have a thought out plan. If
    something changes or you need me, call me. Be
    home Sunday morning by 10 a.m. Have fun. I
    trust your judgment.
Hannah: Great! Thanks, Dad.

The big difference between the fast and slow parenting versions of this conversation is the level of trust. We don't mean trust regarding the teen's behavior, but trust in the teen's judgment. The fast parent is concerned about safety and doesn't trust Hannah to exercise her judgment to meet his standards. Most likely he rarely trusts his daughter, so Hannah is practiced at lying, hiding, deflecting—and slamming the door. The slow parent is concerned about safety, but does trust that Hannah will exercise her judgment and call him if she needs back up. He even asked about her plan. He doesn't support her drinking a beer, and he does want her to call if she needs him. They have created a history of trust because even when she doesn't do what he wants, she's honest about it. She is honest because he doesn't judge her. The slow parent learns the truth right away and knows that Hannah has a plan. The fast parent may never know the truth until it blows up as a crisis.

Slow parents respond to safety issues while building a sustainable relationship with their teenagers. Fast parents earnestly try to keep their teenagers in line, and they're willing to forego a sustainable relationship to assuage their noble fears for safety. As stewards of their teens, slow parents try not to project their selfish fears and do not create rules to box the teenagers in and manage their behavior. The point is to encourage the forest to grow. Teenagers need to learn, discern, be empowered, make mistakes, and exercise their judgment, all with a reliable support system. Slow parents steward their teenagers through these dynamic years, enjoy their teens the whole time, and come out with a relationship that can grow for a lifetime.

EXERCISE

Practicing Stewardship

1. Every day, deliberately look for what is different about your teenager. What's new? Don't judge the change as good or bad, just notice the differences.

   ◆ What new idea has surfaced? What new opinion is expressed?

   ◆ What new friend has appeared? Which old friend left the scene?

   ◆ Is her style of dress a bit different?

   ◆ Are his music choices the same as a month ago?

   ◆ Are her moods what you've come to expect or have they shifted?

   ◆ Has he changed his eating habits in some way?

2. Ask your teenager open ended questions. Let the conversation flow or not—don't push. You're expressing genuine curiosity, not trying for a certain result.

For example:

♦ "Tell me about your day," instead of "Did you have a good day?"

♦ "You seem to be texting your boyfriend a lot today. What's going on?" instead of "Are you two fighting?"

♦ "How can I most help you with your project?" instead of "Did you get your project finished?"

3. Write down a conversation or fight you had with your teenager recently that feels like a fast parenting interaction. Now re-write it from the view point of slow parenting and be curious about your kid. How does it feel different? What did you do or say differently in the new version?

4. Actually have a conversation with your teenager where you're deliberately curious but not judgmental. Practice *not* sharing your opinion or offering advice; just be curious about him and how he thinks and makes choices. How was that for you? Did your teen react differently than usual?

5. Write in your journal about your five biggest safety issues for your teenager. Explore your selfish fears in detail. Ask yourself "So what if this happened?" Look to see if your parenting decisions are motivated by safety or stewardship. Honestly write about your teen's reaction when you parent for her safety. Remember to explore both what you fear for him and what you fear for yourself.

Chapter Five

Attitude Two
-Respect Their Personalities

*"I learned to stop trying to mold my daughter into a
different person and accept her just as she is."*
—Martha L., Colorado Springs

*T*he next Slow Parenting Teens attitude, Respect Their
Personalities, builds on the idea of stewardship. When
you're curious and attentive, you begin noticing who your
teens really are. You see their interests, their priorities, and
the culture they live in. At that point, you can accept the fact
that your teen is a unique and special individual.

When speaking of your teen, we use the word *personality*
to cover a lot of territory: learning and problem solving styles,
interests, tendencies, whether she's thick or thin-skinned,
and whether she's private about her emotions or shares them.
We acknowledge that a teen's personality is a moving target
because teens are always evolving. So when we say "respect
their personalities," we mean "know and accept the teens in
your life as they are, not as you would like them to be, and
not as they were a few months ago."

Your teen's personality also includes whether he processes things internally or externally; he may want to talk things out during a crisis, or he may need quiet time. Friendship and dating are usually priorities for teens, while you'd prefer they focus on school and sports. To respect their personalities, you must respect their interests while taking into account their gender and birth order, along with life events that might include moving, changing schools, an evolving family structure, and experiencing death or other traumatic events. Personality refers to how your teen handles his life.

One of the easiest traps to fall into when you're fast parenting is judging your teenager for being different from you. The world keeps changing; communication and entertainment evolve every day. When you judge and resist texting, reality shows, video games, the Internet, and other new cultural developments, your teenager feels you're judging him. It feels personal. You can set limits on screen time, make requests, and offer options, but don't disapprove of his world. If you want a fun and loving relationship, you must be willing to stretch into his world and stop criticizing it.

What do you find difficult about joining her in her world? Maybe you don't like reality TV shows, but can't you give up an hour of your life now and then to watch a show and spend time with your daughter? Own your fear and make a choice so you can be with your daughter in a positive way. Perhaps you don't want to share her attention with her cell phone. Better to say, "When you're with me, I ask that you don't text," instead of "You text too much."

The challenge in slow parenting attitudes is to remove your parental preference filter. It frankly doesn't matter what you prefer for your teen, if that isn't who and what he is. You may prefer that your son continue studying the violin. After all, you invested money and time in the instrument and lessons, encouraged by the mental image of him playing for a lifetime. But if the violin no longer captures his imagination, it will only become a sore point between you. For the sake of your relationship, keep your preferences out of the conversation. Teenagers are not particularly interested in your preferences, while at the same time, they are keen to not disappoint you. When you interject your own choices for your child, you will skew the relationship. If you truly want to know who your teen is, then you must keep judgment to yourself.

This can be tough if your adolescent is unlike you in a big way. Perhaps you are talkative and she is quiet. Wishing won't make her talk to you more often, and demanding it will not bring happy results. But watching the many nonverbal ways she communicates will give you the information you need. You may not prefer nonverbal communication, but you can learn to respect it. Perhaps you are goal oriented and a list maker, while your daughter is impulsive and less organized. You wish she'd learn to make a list and follow it, as you do. But list-making isn't part of her makeup. You *can* watch to see how she organizes things she wants to complete, and you can support her methods. You might even learn to be more spontaneous. And you can teach her what you do, if and when organization is something she wants to learn. In the meantime, you can watch as natural consequences teach her lessons far better than you would.

Let's look at what it means to respect this multi-layered personality. What does respect look like? So far we've said that parents should avoid judging their teen's personality and culture, but we mean more than that. Respect means being positive about your teen's personality, not undercutting it with sarcasm and pointed humor. You show respect by looking for ideas, music, and apps that might be interesting to your son. Respecting him means watching him, even when you aren't interested in what he's doing. It means staying in a conversation longer than you'd like because he isn't finished. Respect is leaving him alone when you want to talk, but he doesn't. You show respect when you trust that his personality isn't flawed, even if you don't share the same traits and interests. By the time he's a teen, he has a pretty good sense of what's good for him.

To contrast what we're proposing, let's look at how fast parenting tries to change a teen's personality. When you fast parent, you're convinced that shaping your teen's personality is a good thing to do. You may even consider it a primary purpose of parenting. You can explain and rationalize all fast parenting choices because you believe molding your child is your job. While you may be able to manage your teen's behavior, the relationship will suffer. Teens resent unilateral correction, advice, and heavy-handed guidance. Some teens may comply with restrictions and rules, while others will rebel, but they all feel personally attacked and judged. The farthest extreme of this fast parenting behavior happens when you require your teen to agree with your decisions because they're "good for her." If you persist in fast parenting, your teen will show you only the side of her you approve of or she'll throw her differences in your face. Either way, you won't know or appreciate her real personality as she grows and matures. This is *not* how you build a slow parenting relationship.

Slow Parenting Teens advocates remaining curious about who your teenager is and who he's becoming. With slow parenting, you respect his preferences and interests and participate in his activities. You tell him you enjoy sharing time with him and like the way he thinks and forms opinions. Even when you disagree with his opinions, you compliment him on how he reached them. You allow him to make many of his own choices. When you make a decision that affects him, you take into account his unique personality and discuss it with him, if possible.

A benefit of respecting your teen's personality is that she will feel safe coming to you for guidance and input. She will share more of herself, giving you extra opportunities to learn what interests her and how she thinks. You get to see her insights and self-awareness. With this relationship, your teen will come to you to celebrate her successes and you get to join in the celebration.

When you respect your teenager's personality, you cut judgment way, way back, and open the opportunity for more disclosure and fun. When you don't judge your teen, she won't be afraid to come to you. Most parents aren't aware of how damaging their judgments are because they believe offering opinions equals good parenting. We want you to become sensitized to when you judge and its consequences. This is an important part of respecting your teen's personality.

You may be no more proud of your judgments than you are of your selfish fears, but disliking them won't make them go away. Both fear and judgment will undermine the relationship with your teen if you don't recognize them. Only when you acknowledge your judgments can you decide to see past them to your child. All parents judge their teens; that's what we do when we're afraid. However, when you decide to respect your teen's personality, you can choose to look past too much make-up, the boxers hanging out, and the choice to get a C grade because he didn't want to study. You can choose to look past the friend you believe is a bad influence or the sudden decision to quit running track. Respecting her personality relieves you of the responsibility of turning out a perfect kid. Just as trying to keep him safe is impossible, so is turning out a flawless kid. Your parental energy is better spent getting to know your unique teenager and enjoying her.

The examples that follow illustrate how respecting your teen's personality will help you avoid arguments. In the first scenario, a parent and teenager are working out when he will come home from a movie date.

Mom: You may go, but you must be home by midnight.

Jordan: I can't get home by midnight.

Mom: Why not?

Jordan: Well, the movie doesn't get out until 11:30, and I have to take Tiffani home.

Mom: I think you can make it, if you leave as soon as the movie is over, drop Tiffani off, and come straight home.

Jordan: But I may have to give other people a ride home, too.

Mom: Well then, you need to tell them "No" if it means you'll be late.

Jordan: That messes up the whole night and it's not fair! We've planned this all week. I don't understand! What difference could it possibly make if I get back at 12 or 12:30!?

Mom: Enough! Midnight or don't go!

Jordan: Fine.

Here's the same situation with the parent working to respect her son's personality:

Mom: I'd like you home by midnight. I have an early start tomorrow.

Jordan: That isn't going to work. The movie doesn't get out until 11:30, and I still have to take Tiffani home.

Mom: I don't understand why you still can't get home by midnight; Tiffani doesn't live that far away.

Jordan: Yeah, well. I would like some leeway in case things go … ahh… "well" when I drop Tiffani off.

Mom: Oh, that's right, this is your first real date with Tiffani. Got it. Shoot for 12:15 but you won't be in trouble if it's 12:30.

Jordan: Thanks, Mom.

In the fast parenting conversation, Mom is rigid about her rule, and Jordan becomes resentful and dishonest in an effort to manipulate his curfew. The conversation ends in an argument with Mom feeling unappreciated for letting

Jordan go out to begin with, and Jordan feeling frustrated at the unilateral decision imposed upon him. This is a common scenario.

In the slow parenting conversation, Mom owns that the original curfew is for her needs. When Jordan resists the curfew, she's curious about why. Jordan feels comfortable telling her the truth about why he'd like some extra time. Mom empathizes and finds an amicable solution without losing her authority.

In the next example, sex is the hot button. An 18-year-old daughter wishes to go on a camping trip with her friends:

Anna: Dad, can I go camping with some friends this weekend?

Dad: What adults are going?

Anna: None. This is our post-graduation camping party.

Dad: Not going to happen without an adult.

Anna: Dad, I'm 18. I've graduated from high school. So why don't you trust me?

Dad: It's not you I don't trust. This is a situation that could get out of hand really fast. I won't have you going on an unsupervised overnight with boys around.

Anna: You've got to be kidding? I can't go because boys are going?

Dad: That's right.

Anna: I'm leaving for college in 3 months! I won't have supervision there!

Dad: You are not gone, yet! So you can't go.

Anna: I hate you!

The slow parenting conversation goes like this:

Anna: Dad, I'd like to go camping with my friends this weekend.

Dad: Uhmm. Can you tell me more? Where are you going? Any adults? Boys and girls? Your boyfriend?

Anna: Flintridge campgrounds, no adults, and yes, boys
and girls, and my boyfriend.

Dad: Honestly honey, my biggest worry is that you'll be
unsupervised overnight with your boyfriend.

Anna: I understand. And you know me; I'm not going to
have sex in a tent with eight of our friends standing
around. And besides, Dad, we'll be unsupervised
at college soon, anyway.

Dad: I know and you're right. Of course, you can go. I
just want you to make good choices. This is tough
for me.

Anna: Thanks for trusting me, Daddy.

The fast parenting conversation dissolves into a fight
when it doesn't have to. Dad is determined to enforce his
rule and has no interest in Anna's side of the issue or in
considering who she is and her values. In the slow parenting
conversation, both sides explain their positions and listen to
each other. While Dad isn't totally comfortable with Anna's
choice, he learns she has thought things through. She has
personal standards, and he can trust her judgment. She
appreciates his honesty about his concerns and fears, and he
expresses his worry without making it her responsibility.

When parents are open, curious, and accepting of
their teens, they have the privilege of learning what's
going on instead of having events "packaged" for parental
consumption. We hear time and again of teens who won't
tell their parents the truth because they fear judgment,
criticism, or correction. For teens, nothing is more appealing,
engaging, and attractive than someone who's is genuinely
curious about them and trusts their judgment. Respecting
your teens' personality will open a window into their world
you've never had, while giving you the building blocks to
create a strong, sustainable relationship.

EXERCISE
Practicing Respect

1. Tell your teenager you like the way he thinks about
   _____. That's it ... just tell him, with no additions,
   improvements, or corrections. Having parents be curious
   and impressed with their teen and then telling him out
   loud, with no other agenda, is amazingly powerful.

2. Allow and encourage your teenager to make at least three
   decisions a day to which you simply say, "Yes, that's a
   good choice."

3. Celebrate with your teen at least one success a day you had
   nothing to do with. To do this you have to steward. Pay
   attention and notice what your teenager is up to, involved
   in, and with whom she's interacting. Celebrating can be a
   simple "well done," or it may be a gesture your teen will
   appreciate (a movie she wants to see, a special meal, a
   note on his door, or even a status update on Facebook).

4. In your journal, write about the aspects of your teen's
   behavior and personality that drive you crazy or push
   a button for you. Then pick the top three you can't let
   go of and decide to "overlook" the rest from here on.
   Remember, to overlook those traits, you must not take
   them personally.

5. Now write about the aspect and traits of your teen you
   most like and relate to—the things you're proud of and
   want to see more of. These are things to celebrate with
   your teenager and praise him when you notice them.

6. Now honestly write how you judge your teenager, subtle
   or not. You need to be honest with yourself and look for
   your judgments. If you don't think you judge or you aren't
   sure, notice when they start sharing something and then
   abruptly stop. They feel judged. What are you doing?

Are you sarcastic? Do you "tease" your teenager? What about your non-verbal communication: do you roll your eyes, make faces, or avoid eye contact? You may think she doesn't feel judged by you, but do you listen to her solutions and then add your own? Do you offer advice when he hasn't asked? Do you praise her choice but then improve upon it? Do you ask him what he wants and then proceed to tell him why that isn't a good thing? Do you flat out tell her she's wrong, or she made a stupid choice? Do you not believe him when he apologizes? Do you say things like, "Are you kidding?" or "What were you thinking?"

If you don't know how your judgment reveals itself, then it will be hard to change. If you aren't sure, ask your teen!

Chapter Six

Attitude Three
-Catch Them Doing It Right

"You catch more flies with honey than with vinegar."
—Old Adage

*I*n general, parents point out to their teens the things they do wrong. This is so common that it's a habit. We encourage parents to change their focus and to Catch Them Doing It Right. Fast parents expend enormous amounts of time and energy correcting, criticizing, and punishing teens for behavior, dress, attitude, study habits, and friends. The justification for pointing out what teens do wrong is to better equip them and prepare them for adulthood. On the surface, this seems like a noble goal. Fast parents believe that pointing out what a teen does wrong or could do better is not only helpful, but necessary for good parenting.

Unfortunately, what a teen hears isn't helpful advice, but rather an avalanche of negativity, and he shuts down. It would eventually shut down anyone to be constantly told how he could improve, but your teenager is especially sensitive to what you say and think. After a while, he assumes that when you want to talk to him, he will be corrected. Whether your comment is couched as feedback or spoken nicely, he hears criticism and judgment and becomes resentful, hurt, or simply turns off. He is on guard, defensive, and will not share openly with you. Thus begins the lie, hide, minimize, and deny cycle to avoid your judgment and keep from being in trouble.

Even when a fast parent gives a compliment before suggesting how the teenager could do it better the next time, the teen only hears criticism, "You didn't do it quite right the first time." The compliment is completely lost. Whatever your intention, you just caught her doing it wrong. Maybe she didn't do something the way you think she should have, and perhaps she'll face unpleasant consequences, but is it worth undermining your relationship?

Even when you gently point out what he did wrong or could do better, you do his work for him and hinder his development. He doesn't develop his own ability to connect his behavior with the natural consequences. Instead, he focuses on your reaction and defending his actions. Think about it. Inevitably, when you tell a teen what he could have done better, he either explains or justifies his action (which leads to a fight) or he shuts down and doubts himself. He doesn't need to look at the natural consequences of his actions because his field of vision is taken up by you. You redirected his attention to defending himself or to beating himself up. Either way, this isn't good for your relationship.

Slow Parenting Teens is all about building a relationship. Catching Them Doing It Right is critical to keeping lines of communication open, so you can build that relationship. When you catch her doing something right, you also have the opportunity to celebrate how she made her decision. You get to hear that she considered a variety of choices and she's aware of her motivations and challenges. Catching her doing it right helps you appreciate her personality and better steward her. We ask you to appreciate everything your teen does right, no matter how small, and no matter the final outcome. When you do, your teenager will turn to you more often and expand the opportunities to add your guidance.

This requires some rethinking on your part about what's right. Right doesn't always mean, "the way I would do it," and it doesn't always mean the outcome is what you had in mind. Right, in this case, means he has thought through situations, taken responsibility, made purposeful and informed choices, and seen his part in the outcome. Right is when he makes *any* effort to complete his chores, follow the rules, or do what he was asked. Right is when he takes initiative, attempts to solve his own problems, handles situations by himself, or asks for help when he needs it. Your teenager is constantly doing something right. Your job is to notice it.

You have to *develop* this skill because you've been trained to do the opposite: notice what isn't right and what isn't working. People usually look for what can be improved upon and take for granted the times when things are going well and working as they should. That's okay if it's your car, and it's running well. You don't have to thank your car for starting every day, but with your teenager, nothing is a given. Slow parents take nothing for granted. Everything is an opportunity to build a positive relationship with your teen. This is all about deciding to change your focus and catch her doing things right.

Here are examples of what we mean: When your son isn't swearing anymore after you asked him to quit, notice it. When your daughter wears a tank top under a low cut shirt, compliment her. When he takes out the trash after having been asked only three times, thank him without even a hint of sarcasm. Notice when she leaves her phone in her pocket during dinner. Anytime your teen does something right, notice it.

The major benefit for Catching Them Doing Right is that you will change your perspective of your teenager.

You'll focus on who your teen is and what he does, instead of who he isn't and what he doesn't do. When you're alert to what your teen does right, you'll learn to appreciate his personality and talents. Also, it's much more fun to tell him you noticed something positive; there's less eye rolling, tisking, and exiting the room in a huff—by anyone. Catching her doing it right helps create a safe arena for your teen to be a work in progress. He knows you aren't judging him and you're paying attention to more than the bad stuff, which in turn creates a positive, sustainable relationship between you.

Another payoff of this attitude is that teens often change how they view themselves. When you catch your teen doing it right, she sometimes starts catching herself doing things right. She notices the positive steps she's taking in her life, which can help her build confidence and self-esteem. She may even pass on the compliment by noticing what other people are doing right. She starts noticing effort and intention in the actions of those around her, not just the outcome. In short, she may start appreciating you and your efforts as well.

When you fast parent, catching them doing it right is hard because you're trained to automatically notice how things can be improved upon. Even if your teen is doing something well, it can always be better. You fear that if you aren't correcting your teenager or offering ways for her to improve, you aren't being a good parent. This often reveals your selfish fear of being judged by others—teachers and other parents. If you're afraid of being labeled a bad parent, then understand that this fear may be your underlying motive for correcting your teen. Own it, own it, own it. And then review your intentions for your relationship with your child. If you want a slow parenting relationship, start catching her doing it right.

The truth is, you will still offer your teen advice and correction. Even the slowest of slow parents give unsolicited feedback. However, we want you to notice if you're trying to mold your teen's behavior with your advice. You can easily slip into using positive feedback as a tool to manipulate your teen. Think of training a puppy or rats in a maze. For example, if you compliment your teen on doing a chore so she'll do the chore without being asked next time, then you're attached to the outcome and trying to manipulate her. If, instead, you genuinely compliment her for taking out the trash and you have no additional motive or expectation, then you aren't attached to the outcome, and there is no manipulation. Teens see right through your manipulations; they feel your motivation long before you do.

Manipulation doesn't build a relationship. The way to test your motivation is to notice if you're angry, disappointed, resentful, or attached in any way to having your teenager take your advice. When your teen says, "no," if you still try to sell your idea or convince her in another way, then you must back off, because you're attached to the outcome and manipulating. Slow parents are not attached to the outcomes of their teen's behavior; fast parents are. Slow parents don't try to manipulate their teens; fast parents do.

The following scenarios illustrate the difference between a slow parent catching a teenager doing it right and a fast parent catching him doing it wrong. In the first case, a teen's friend has just been suspended from school for having smoked marijuana in the park across the street. Let's start with the fast parent:

Dad: I just heard about your friend, Steve. You aren't hanging out with him ever again.

Peter: That isn't fair; I didn't do anything wrong.

Dad: He's a bad influence. I don't trust him. This is not up for discussion.

Peter: Dad, you don't even know what happened.

Dad: I know he got suspended for smoking pot. That's all I need to know.

Peter: What has that got to do with me? Why am I being punished? Don't you trust me?

Dad: No, not if you think it's okay to hang out with somebody like him. I don't trust you.

Peter: If you restrict me from hanging out with everyone
who gets stoned, I won't have any friends.

Dad: That's okay with me, since you obviously have
lousy judgment picking friends.

Peter: This is ridiculous. You're flipping out, and I didn't
do anything wrong.

Dad: If you keep hanging out with Steve, you will. This
conversation is over.

A slow parenting conversation might go like this:

Dad: Wow, I just heard about Steve. Tell me what
happened.

Peter: Well, you know Steve sometimes smokes pot.
Yesterday he asked me if I wanted to go to the
park with him at lunch while he got high. I tried
to talk him out of it because it was a dumb idea,
but he went anyway and got caught.

Dad: I'm really proud of you for not going with him.
You made a good choice. You could have gotten
in trouble too.

Peter: I know! And then I would have missed math and
practice. I'm not doing that for anyone.

Dad: Are you concerned about Steve smoking pot?

Peter: Sometimes, but I've stopped hanging out with him
when he's smoking.

Dad: Sounds like you've thought this through. Thanks
for telling me what happened.

These conversations illustrate the maxim that parents
find what they're looking for. The fast parenting dad couldn't
imagine Peter had done anything right. He parented from his
own fears. Dad's fears overrode all other parenting choices
and showed up as a unilateral decision that discounted Peter's
judgment. Dad has damaged his relationship with his son.

The slow parent started by expecting to catch Peter
doing it right. By inviting Peter to explain the situation and

give his perspective, Dad opened the possibility of catching him doing it right. Dad acknowledged his fear and was able to recognize Peter's good judgment. The slow parent's conversation focused on Peter's positive actions in a difficult situation; the fast parent conversation focused on Peter's bad judgment for being Steve's friend. One built the relationship; the other tore it down.

Here's another set of fast and slow parenting dialogues that illustrate the idea of catching them doing it right. This scenario involves a ninth grade boy and his mother. She was looking for socks in his drawer and found a condom:

Mom: Andrew, we have to talk. Immediately.

Andrew: What now?

Mom: What is *this condom* doing in your dresser drawer?

Andrew: You were in my dresser?

Mom: That isn't what we're here to talk about. What are you doing with a condom?

Andrew: Nothing. A friend gave it to me.

Mom: Are you having sex? You are only 14! Why are you even thinking about having sex!?

Andrew: Calm down! I am not having sex!

Mom: You'd better not be! You know how I feel about teenagers having sex. It's dangerous and wrong!

Andrew: I KNOW, I KNOW! I am not having sex. I don't even have a girlfriend.

Mom: Well, if you have a condom, then you're thinking about having it and not respecting this family's values about premarital sex. This tells me I need to watch you more carefully.

Andrew: That is totally unfair. I am not having sex; I haven't done anything wrong. And now I'm in trouble.

Mom: Darn right you're in trouble. I don't trust your judgment.

The slow parenting version of the conversation goes like this:

Mom: Andrew, I need to talk to you for a minute.

Andrew: Okay. What's up?

Mom: Well, I want to apologize. I was putting away your laundry and went into your sock drawer without your permission. I found this condom.

Andrew: Oh. Huh.

Mom: I will never go into your drawers again. I want to respect your privacy. But I do need to point something out.

Andrew: What?

Mom: I realize you're thinking about sex, and I'm glad to know you're thinking about protection and birth control at the same time. That shows me you have good judgment around this important issue. But I need to point out that this particular condom is past its expiration date.

Andrew: Oh, wow. I … am not having sex.

Mom: Okay, that's great. I'm glad you aren't sexually active at 14. I think you're making a good choice. I don't want you to have sex before you're ready. And I definitely know I'm not ready for you being sexually active. But when you feel ready, just don't use *this* condom.

Andrew: Okay, Mom. Are we done?

Mom: Yes. Just know I'm here.

The fast parent assumes Andrew is doing something wrong. A condom is a sign of potential misbehavior, and she's upset with him for something that hasn't happened yet. She punishes Andrew by increasing her surveillance, so she can continue to catch him doing it wrong. She's so afraid of Andrew's potential sexual activity that she doesn't consider he may have forgotten about the condom or took it from his friend to save face. She's certain he's doing it all wrong, and perfectly willing to punish him for the conclusion she reached. With this exchange, the mom has made all future conversations about sex much more difficult.

In contrast, the slow parenting mom leaves the door open for further dialogue while complimenting Andrew's current choices around his sexuality. She does not assume a condom equals sexually activity. She asks and believes him when he answers. She acknowledges and praises his decision to not be sexually active at 14. She doesn't punish or criticize him for future choices. She catches him doing it right, right now.

When you point out what your teen could do better, all she hears is correction and criticism. She stops listening because she anticipates all interaction will be about correction and blame, no matter what. Pointing out what she does wrong inhibits a fun, easy relationship, so talk about what she does right, and then see how she begins to enjoy talking with you.

EXERCISE
How to Catch Them Doing it Right

1. Look for at least five things your teenager is doing right each day and tell her you notice. Track this for two weeks.

   Did you struggle to find five things? Did you get sidetracked by noticing the negatives? Did you notice but didn't say anything? What seems different about interactions with your teen after two weeks of this practice?

2. Now ask yourself, "Do I assume my kid has a thought-out rationale for his choices, or do I assume he's making choices on the fly and without thinking them through?"

   The answer will tell you if you're in the habit of catching him doing it right or wrong. Be honest with yourself. If you habitually catch him doing it wrong, we guarantee your attitude is negatively affecting your relationship.

3. What does *right* mean to you? Is your teen doing it right if she gets the outcome you want? Is she right only if it's

your way? Is it right if she puts thought and effort into something, no matter how it turns out? Is it right if she takes the initiative? Is it right if she asked for help? Is it right if she didn't ask for help? Is it right that the task got done, but not in a timely way or to your standards?

4. Use your journal to answer these questions about you:
   What things do you intentionally do to increase your teen's self-esteem?
   What do you do that undermines your teen's confidence and self-esteem?
   How have you manipulated or attempted to manipulate your teen's behavior and choices?

Chapter Seven

Attitude Four
–Listening is Effective

"I don't argue with my Mom because she always listens.
That doesn't mean I get my way, but we just don't fight."
—Hannah, 14 yrs old

As a rule of thumb, we think parents should give up lecturing to teenagers. Teens immediately pick up the "lecture voice" and switch off their ears, no matter what the topic. Often a lecture is a version of, "If I tell you my story ad nauseum, you will see it my way." Lectures are a form of coercion, not discussion. Your lecture is about you telling your story, not about listening to your teen's story. Such one-sidedness will not help you build a relationship with your teen. We suggest you replace lecturing with listening.

So why do you bother to lecture? If you're fast parenting, you think your experience and reasoning are going to influence your teen's choices and behavior. If that doesn't work, the force of repetition will make her see the world through your eyes. You believe you understand your teen's experience and that she'll benefit from your input. You may justify lecturing by saying you're saving her from mistakes and teaching her about how to live life better and with fewer consequences.

Lecturing is risky for several reasons. First, lectures take the focus off the teen and put it on you—your story, your preferences, your opinions, and your interpretations. When it's all about you, you take attention away from your teen, and teens need a lot of attention. Remember, your relationship is 80 percent about him; there's no equality here. So if your teen hasn't asked for any of this information about you, his reaction to the lecture is to get angry, defensive, or shut down. Your lecture will not build an open, fun, loving, and respectful relationship.

The more you develop a slow parenting relationship, the more your teenager will ask for your input. Still, your relationship is 80 percent to 20 percent in their favor, so keep your input short and get the focus back on him.

Lecturing is also dangerous because it implies your teen has done something wrong or *will* do something wrong. Teens get defensive and argue when they feel accused. A fight is a sure sign you haven't been listening. You don't have to agree with your teen, but you do need to respectfully listen to her reasoning. If you use lectures to criticize in advance what you assume she's thinking about doing, you have resorted to threats. This scolding-in-advance is about your selfish fears. You're afraid of your teen's choices and how these choices will ultimately affect you. You can manage your teen's behavior with threats and punishment, but threats will damage your long term relationship.

If you have a pattern of lecturing after a deed is done, then the lectures become a form of punishment. Most people will avoid punishment if possible, and teenagers are no exception. To avoid your lecture, your teen will do whatever he can to make sure you never discover what actually happened. And he will hide what he's planning to do. At best, you'll get a watered down version of events. You may be more comfortable with the watered down version, but it isn't honest—it's your teen managing your fears for you. To make you feel less afraid and thus avoid your lecture, teens will perfect their skills in lying, hiding, and denying. As far as slow parenting teens is concerned, lecturing is a no win strategy. Lecturing does nothing for developing a lasting and positive relationship with a teenager.

Listening, the way we refer to it, means your teenager's story is more important than your story. You want to hear her process, conclusions, questions, logic, and confusion. Then you'll ask for more of her thoughts at least two times before you even venture a remark, much less an opinion. This is a delicate skill that takes time to perfect, but it's worth the effort because your teen will actually start using you as a sounding board, telling you what's going on, and allowing you to be in a close relationship with her. She'll turn to you if she's in trouble and seek your input and feedback because she knows you won't judge, correct, or subject her to a list of your own experiences.

You can easily fall into traps when you first begin listening to your teen. For example, you might piggyback on her information and bring the discussion back to *you* in an attempt to show how much you understand what she's sharing. All that does is highjack the conversation and make it about you. Another subtle way to not listen is to interrupt her with a question. We're all conditioned to stop our train of thought and answer a question, and then the conversation goes in that direction. Your question's direction is probably not where the teen was headed had you kept your mouth closed, and now you'll never know what he was going to tell you.

Real listening is deeply respectful. You gather information about who your teen is when he tells you about what he's doing and thinking. You'll get more opportunities to catch him doing lots of things right. Listening is effective because it enhances the other attitudes of Slow Parenting Teens. You can tell you're listening well when the phrase, "yes, but..." never crosses your lips.

Granted, you won't always be fascinated by what your teen wants to talk about. We still encourage you to listen to everything your teen is willing to share, even if you aren't interested. Especially if you aren't interested. This kind of listening gives you the chance to be curious and to find out what he likes and why he likes it. And when something he says brings up fear for you, notice your fears. When he finishes sharing with you, go to work on those fears in your journal or with another adult. This kind of listening is especially important if your teen isn't a big talker. When he does share, listen to him carefully and with curiosity.

This kind of listening sets the stage for your teenager to let you know what's really going on. You create a safe, accepting space where she can explore different ideas, be confused, contradict herself, and find her way to new ideas and solutions with you as a safety net. Learning to listen well is challenging; it requires you to unlearn the lecturing habit and hear about things you may not want to know. We believe Dave Ellis, author and leadership coach, when he says, "The quality of your relationship is in direct proportion to the quality of your listening."

Sometimes your teenager needs to talk, but the timing is inconvenient for you. You can certainly put limits on the time you have available or schedule another time to listen. But when you're listening, remember to do absolutely nothing else. Give your teen your undivided attention. And if you can't offer undivided attention, tell your teen you can only give him part of your attention. He can decide if partial attention is good enough. For example, when you're driving in the car together, you get a chance to listen, but you can't give your teen 100 percent of your attention. Ask if that's okay or if you should wait until you can listen without multi-tasking.

Perhaps your teenager doesn't talk much, or maybe you have one who won't stop as long as she has an audience. Each young person has her own way of communicating, and your job is to accommodate and respect your teen's personality. If you have a teen who doesn't talk often, when she does open up you should drop everything to listen, if at all possible. If you have a teen who talks incessantly, it's okay to put limits on your time. Each is a way of stewarding your teen, as long as you're genuinely curious and paying attention.

Listening means being attentive, asking the question "what else?", and giving feedback only when asked. You listen without planning what to say next, and you don't hurry your teen to "get to the point." This kind of listening is hard; it requires focus and patience. Remember, building a trusting relationship with your teen is absolutely worth your time and effort.

When you start listening this way, we guarantee you'll hear things that bring up your fears. You'll learn about something her friends did, an activity she thinks is exciting that seems scary to you, choices she's considering, or choices she's already made that you disagree with. At the least, you'll be worried; at worst, you'll be terrified. Be prepared and try to not take over the conversation, no matter how freaked out you are. Stay in the conversation until she's done, and then handle your fears with another adult. Perhaps you'll need to come back to your teen at a later time to talk about what you're afraid of or to set limits, but keep your fear to yourself during the initial conversation.

We'd like to mention a few other things to avoid when listening to your teenager. Please be careful not to use adult versions of eye rolling, tisking, and other judgmental, non-verbal communication. You hate it when they do it to you, and they hate it, too. Also don't break his confidentiality, even if he didn't specifically request it. If you feel the need to share something your teen has told you, check with him first, invite him to do the sharing, and always use extreme care.

Finally, do not use against him something he shared openly and honestly with you. If you need to set limits around something he shared, then please do so sooner rather than later, and while you're doing it, own that it's about you—not him. If you wait, he may feel you're storing up ammunition against him, and he'll stop talking to you.

When you listen well, your teen will feel safe with you because you aren't telling her what to do, correcting her, or judging her actions. She will be more honest with you because she doesn't have to protect you. You will be a safe place for her to sort out her confusion and make tough decisions. She gets lots of praise and compliments from you on how she handles life, and she feels comforted when she makes mistakes. You want your teen doing all this while you can be there as a safety net. She might even get to brag that she doesn't have to lie to her parents. She'll make choices for herself that take you into account, lovingly and respectfully. This is the sustainable relationship we have been promising you.

We know that the more you listen, the more they'll share. Teenagers just want to be listened to! Marti, as a former adolescent therapist, often surprised parents when she told them that a reluctant teen had talked for the whole hour. The parents couldn't get the kid to talk at all. When asked how she did it, she replied, "I listened and was curious."

What does all this listening look like? The following dialogues are between a dad and his 13-year-old daughter about her relationship with her friends. Here's a fast parenting conversation:

Dad: Why have you been so moody lately?

Angie: I haven't been moody. What are you talking about?

Dad: You snap at me when I ask you a question. I asked about your day at school and you rolled your eyes, and you just made a disgusting noise while texting your friend.

Angie: Okay, fine. I am in a bad mood, but Mary is talking trash behind Suzie's back, and Suzie is texting me to find out what's going on with Mary. I don't want to get in the middle because this happens between them all the time.

Dad (sighs): I'm really sick of this. I want you to tell both of them you aren't going to be friends with them anymore. You need to hang out with people who are supportive. I had a friend at your age who always talked bad about people, and I ended getting in trouble because everyone thought I was part of it. The best thing you can do right now is stop talking to both of them until they grow up, if they ever grow up! You definitely have to quit taking this out on the family; it isn't fair to us.

Angie: Dad—Mary and Suzie have been my two best friends since kindergarten. I'm not going to dump them. That's ridiculous. And I'm not the only one around here who gets in a bad mood!

Dad: Well, when you take your mood out on us, it's disrespectful.

Angie: Well, what about you and your moods?

Dad: Young lady, don't you talk to me that way. I'm your father, and I was just trying to help.

Angie: Fine. Arghhhh.

And she's out of the room in a flash.

The slow parenting version of the conversation goes like this:

Dad: Are you alright? You seem preoccupied.

Angie: Yeah. It's just friend drama, again.

Dad: Tell me about it. What's going on?

Angie: Well, Mary is talking trash behind Suzie's back, and Suzie is texting me to find out what's going on with Mary. I don't want to get in the middle because this happens between them all the time.

Dad: You sound frustrated. What else is going on?

Angie: Well, I am frustrated. They're both my friends

and I'm not going to pick sides. I can see where they're both coming from, but I have no idea how to stay out of this.

Dad: Tell me what you've tried already.

Angie: I told them I don't want to be in the middle, and I wasn't going to answer their texts. And they both got mad at me. If I hang out with one of them, the other is mad at me. I just can't win.

Dad: What else?

Angie: Well, the only time I managed to get out from between these two before is when I refused to hang out with either of them until they got along. That was hard because they're both stubborn. But now that I think about it, I spent time with friends I hadn't seen for awhile. So maybe I'll try that again.

Dad: Sounds like a good idea. I'm proud of your for not picking sides and for coming up with a creative solution. Will you tell me how it turns out?

Angie: Yeah, and I am sorry I've been moody.

Dad: No biggie. Thanks for telling me what's going on.

See how easy this is? We know it may seem hard at first, but soon this process will feel natural. Listening and supporting your teen is as simple as saying, "Tell me more," staying curious, and trusting she can find her own solutions. You might think giving advice is helping, but it's just another form of lecturing—and teens recognize this even before you do. We guarantee they will shut down or defend when you lecture. A shut-down is your cue that you haven't been listening, and it's time to try again.

Here's a situation in which a college student calls home to tell his father the school will be calling about a party in the dorm where they were all cited for underage drinking.

Steve: Dad, I'm calling to let you know the college will be contacting you to tell you I've been cited for underage drinking.

Dad: What the hell are you talking about? What do you mean cited?

Steve: It means the police were called, and I got a ticket.

Dad: Why is the school calling me?

Steve: Because it happened on campus—and I might be suspended.

Dad: @#$#$%^%$##!!! I knew this was going to happen. Bunch of college kids, thinking the rules don't apply. Well, we're here now, so here's what to do. You need to meet with the dean, write an apology letter, distance yourself from those kids, and if you need an attorney, you'll be paying for that, rest assured. What were you thinking?

Steve: Dad, can't we just wait until you hear from the college?

Dad: No, we have to get ahead of this.

Steve: I don't know what's going to happen.

Dad: Well, I do. We have to make sure this isn't on your academic record and or any other record. I just can't believe you've screwed up already!

Steve: Calm down, Dad. This isn't the end of the world. I think the college has been through this before. They aren't looking to suspend 20 freshmen.

Dad: That cavalier attitude is going to screw up your college career. I expect you not to drink another drop of alcohol until you're 21!

Steve: Dad, that's ridiculous.

Dad: I've been to college. I know about the partying, and I warned you about this. If you had just listened to me! But you didn't listen to me, so now you're going to do it my way!

Steve: Fine, Dad.

Now, here is the slow parenting version of the phone call home:

Steve: Dad, I'm calling to let you know the college will be calling to tell you I've been cited for underage drinking.

Dad: Tell me what happened.

Steve: Well, okay. Our hall had a party and we were drinking. It got a little loud. The campus cops came to see what was going on, and they called the police.

Dad: Must have been very loud.

Steve: Yeah, and a couple of kids got belligerent with the campus cops, too.

Dad: So then what happened?

Steve: It was pretty obvious we'd all been drinking, so they checked ID's and wrote all twenty of us tickets. This morning we all got an email from the Dean of Students saying they had decided to contact our parents.

Dad: Are they talking about suspending you?

Steve: I don't know, yet. We all have meetings with the dean's office scheduled for Monday.

Dad: How are you doing?

Steve: I'm really bummed, and I'm disappointed in myself. Honestly, Dad, I never thought of the consequences until they happened.

Dad: Yeah, I understand that. What else?

Steve: I'm scared because I don't know what's going to happen. I don't know how much the ticket is going to be, or if I'll have other legal things to deal with. And technically I could be suspended. I hope the school has another way of handling this; they've been through it before.

Dad: Sounds like you're taking responsibility, and I think you're right that the school probably doesn't want to suspend twenty of you. Anything else?

Steve: Well, I'm ready to handle whatever consequences come: pay the fine and take care of what comes from the school. I think I've got it, now.

Dad: Thanks for telling me, and it sounds like you've got things under control. I'm sorry you have to go through this. I'm here if you need to talk some more.

Steve: I know, Dad, and thanks a lot. A lot of my friends were terrified to call their parents; I was just really embarrassed.

Dad: Let's keep in touch as things unfold. I love you.

Steve: I love you, too.

When Dad listens, the son talks. In the fast parenting scenario, Dad never let Steve explain what happened or take responsibility and ownership for his actions. The conversation is all about Dad's fear and anger. He jumps in with preemptive directions before either of them knows what will be needed. Fast parents give advice and directions, never letting teens learn to do it themselves. And the fast parents are often wrong. Also notice Steve didn't want to stay in the conversation. He called out of obligation and tolerated his dad until he could get off the phone.

The slow parenting scenario has Steve talking much more than Dad. By being quiet, Dad finds out more of what's going on and how Steve is taking responsibility for the situation and learning some lessons. The school and the police will provide plenty of discipline and consequences; Dad chooses to remain in the relationship and be a safe place for his son to talk.

Teenagers will talk when their parents listen. When parents lecture, they miss the opportunity to learn about their teen and build a positive relationship. Adolescents are in a self-focused developmental stage, and most learn through experience, not from someone else's stories — even yours. To listen well, parents must be genuinely curious about their children's situations, feelings, thought processes, problem solving efforts, and desires. We urge you to practice listening well to your teens, so you can better steward them, respect their personalities, and catch them doing it right.

EXERCISE
Ways to Practice Listening

1. How do you define lecturing? Is lecturing the same as punishing? How did you feel about being lectured when you were a teen?

2. Would you rather hear the truth or a lie from your teenager, if the truth is going to scare you? If you said the truth, then do you make it safe for your teen to tell you the truth?

3. Are you guilty of lecturing?
   How do you lecture? Do you interrupt her and tell her how much you understand because you had a similar experience? Do you stand over him and force him to sit while you tell him everything he did wrong? Do you guilt her by telling her how her choices and behavior hurt you? Do you insist he be respectful and say "yes, sir" and apologize? Do you cry while describing in detail how she hurt your feelings? Do you share your wisdom and experience because you've been there and want him to learn from your mistakes?

4. Now about your listening skills...
   ♦ What percentage of the time do you listen to your teenager?
   ♦ What percentage do you think is best for a great relationship?
   ♦ Do you listen to solve the problem or fix the situation?
   ♦ What response do you typically get when you try to fix the situation?

◆ Does that kind of listening further the conversation or shut it down?

5. For the next week or so, when your teen shares, practice saying only "what else?" and "tell me more about that" and see what happens. Track the results in your journal.

6. Notice the ways you interrupt your teenager...
   ◆ Do you ask questions?
   ◆ Do you say "uh huh" a lot?
   ◆ Do you speak before he's finished with the sentence?
   ◆ Do you interject how much you understand?

7. To help you remember to listen well...
   ◆ Handle distractions before you listen.
   ◆ Don't ask leading questions.
   ◆ Be extremely careful not to piggy back or highjack the conversation (don't make it about you).
   ◆ Listen to learn about your teenager, not to fix the problem.
   ◆ Remember, you can and should invite your teen to share and talk, but respect her choice not to, if that's what she decides—just keep inviting her.

Chapter Eight

Attitude Five
-Parent Every Day

"It's easy to share with my mom when she asks about specific people and events in my life. I know she's curious and really is interested, so I want to share even more and hear her opinions."
—Maggie, age 17

Sometimes parenting every day is difficult, but parents must find ways to have consistent interaction with their teens. Teenagers gradually become autonomous: they arrange their school lives, pick their own clothes, manage their time, and are able to get around. Eventually they drive themselves. They turn more toward their friends, think for themselves, make decisions you don't even know about, and often have busy, active lives to manage. They don't need you in the ways they have before, and they seem to be fine. This can be freeing for you, and when your life gets busy as well, you may be tempted to pull back and give your teen less attention—especially when you don't have a slow parenting relationship and your teen is keeping you at arm's length. At such times, it's easy to lose the habit of regular communication. No matter how your daily schedule changes, we urge you to parent every day.

When you aren't in the habit of regular communication, you tend to parent by crisis. When a big event occurs, you show up with your fast parenting tools, ready to attack the problem or the teen. You react to the crisis without taking time to consider your own selfish fears or the relationship you have with your son or daughter. Your contact with your teen becomes about the crisis, not about the relationship. When there's no crisis, you sometimes don't show up at all. If the only way your teen is sure to get your attention is by having a crisis, then there will be a crisis.

While leaving the teen alone seems to support his autonomy, it is really the ultimate fast parenting: in and out, no lingering conversation, handle the issue, and move on. You make all the decisions about solving the crisis; your teen is expected to simply comply. Consequences are handed out. The crisis is over, and everyone goes back to their own lives. You stay out of your teen's life in the name of letting him make his own decisions. However, if a problem arises, you leap in with solutions that don't allow him to make his own decisions. Because you're working in the fast parenting mode, your solutions are often based on your selfish fears, followed by lectures that point out what your teen did wrong.

We know you're busy. You often have to arrange your life so that non-parenting priorities come first and parenting comes second. This seems appropriate because of the autonomy level of your teen, and she isn't seeking you out anyway. We understand the dilemmas of working parents, parents who are in school, parents with other care-giving responsibilities, and so on. Nonetheless, we request that you make parenting your top priority, even if that means simply inviting your teenager to have a ten-minute, focused conversation every day.

When you limit interaction to when something goes wrong, then your teen has only negative feedback for guidance and is less likely to turn to you for help. Teens will turn to other teens for guidance and understanding, which often becomes the blind leading the blind. Also your teen can get involved in serious situations that quickly spiral out of control. When you don't parent every day, it becomes easy to minimize a serious problem as "typical teenage behavior." When you don't have an ongoing relationship and you want to talk with your teen, you may find you have nothing to talk about, or the conversation turns into a fight. Teens who are left to their own devices naturally distrust you when you decide you suddenly want a conversation or a relationship. You didn't seem to care yesterday, why do you care today? It feels to him as if you're just handling a situation or managing his behavior, not trying to build a relationship. Slow parenting is about parenting every day—whether there's trouble or whether there's just life.

Parenting every day brings many pay offs. If it's easy for your teenager to have meaningful conversations with you, you'll have a chance to see how her thinking evolves, what pressures she feels, the joys she experiences, and what opportunities are opening for her. Every day parenting makes this knowledge of your teen the status quo, not a special occasion. If your teenager wants your attention, she knows you'll find an opportunity to talk. Often those talks lead to problem solving sessions that keep at least some crises at bay.

Yes, teens are more autonomous, more private, their friends are more important, and they may react as if you're ripping off their digits when you ask to spend time with them, but your invitation is important. Teens send the "back off" message all the time; don't be daunted. Continue to say, "I like you, I want to know what is going on with you, you are my priority." Say "I want to have a conversation with you, no matter what your mood or attitude. You don't have to be a certain way for me to love you. I love you just as you are."

To do this, you need to remember that everything you do is personal, but nothing they do is personal. While they will interpret your body language, tone of voice, and facial expressions as judgmental comments on them, don't you take it personally when they do something to you, including moods, eye rolling, silence, arguing, heavy sighs, and pulling away. Even if their actions do have something to do with you, they're a diversion. Don't take the bait. You end up fighting about his rude behavior and miss the opportunity to hear what he would have shared. So even if your teen pushes you away, err on the side of parenting every day, even as she gripes that you're parenting too much. Parenting every day means consistently offering your teenager the opportunity to be in conversation with you, whether he takes you up on it or not.

By parenting every day, we do not mean planning and organizing, multitasking, figuring out family logistics, or arguing. We do mean catching him doing something right, listening, learning something about him that wasn't there yesterday, and making eye contact. It may involve hugging, snuggling, sitting on the edge of a bed, doing things together, or meeting for ice cream or a meal. Parenting every day is about remembering what's going on in your teen's life and asking about it from a place of curiosity, not accountability. Every day, create the time and space for a genuine conversation where you ask her what she wants or needs from you. To build a sustainable, fun, and respectful relationship, it has to be mostly about her, not you. Parent every day, whether she wants you to or not.

As a parent you must remain curious about what your teen is doing and thinking. You must persist past the stiff arm, the blithe "I'm fine," and even the blatant, "Get out of my life," to stay in conversation with your teen. You don't have to be in his face, but be around and have regular, reliable contact so he'll continue to have a safe place to just be who he is, infuriating as that may be at times. A slammed bedroom door after school isn't the end of the day. Give your teen time to regroup and start fresh. Let the next conversation stand on its own merit and not be colored by the slammed door. Take each opportunity to connect as it comes and create more if you need to.

This is especially important once your teen becomes mobile and can drive or travel alone. Your windows of opportunity will begin to look like mail slots. Make them count so you can stay connected. You absolutely cannot do it all on the weekend or during some other time you've planned. Your teen has plans, too, and they really are more important to her than you are right now. When you parent every day, you extend the invitation for a conversation over and over, whether she lives with you or not, is away at college, or traveling with a team; it's your responsibility to extend that invitation.

The following scenarios show the difference between parenting every day and parenting only in a crisis. This teenager is failing math.

> Mom: Your math teacher called today and told me you have an F in her class. You're grounded until that grade is at least a C.
>
> Jacob: Why do you care? It's my grade. You don't care about anything else.
>
> Mom: I care when you embarrass me. I hate to get these calls. I have to take time out of my day—just drop everything to deal with a call I shouldn't even be getting. Now your school thinks I am a bad parent!
>
> Jacob: You are a bad parent! I asked you to help me with my math homework three times, and you told me it was my problem.
>
> Mom: How dare you make this about me? You know how much I have to work. And your little brother needs my time. You're a teenager; you should have asked your teacher for help.

Jacob: I told you last week, she only gives that help after school, and you said I have to be here to babysit.

Mom: Well, that's ridiculous. Just figure it out some other way. I don't want another call, so you're grounded until you get your grade up.

Jacob: Right, like you're going to be around to enforce that one!

The slow parenting version of this conversation goes like this:

Mom: I got a call from your math teacher today; he's concerned about the F you have and wanted to make sure I'm aware of it. I told him I am and that you have a plan to bring the grade up. Apparently, sweetheart, your plan isn't working.

Jacob: Yeah. I was really hoping my plan would work. But it didn't – at least not yet.

Mom: Well, do you want a new plan?

Jacob: Yeah. The teacher holds an afternoon help class. I'd like to go, but I know you need me to babysit.

Mom: How much time do you think you'll need to pull up your grade?

Jacob: Probably a couple of weeks.

Mom: I'm willing to make different arrangements for your little brother, but I'm going to check in with you every day.

Jacob: That's fair. When can I start?

Mom: Let's aim for the end of the week.

Jacob: Thanks for going out of your way and helping me out.

Mom: No problem.

The fast parent has no idea what was happening in Jacob's life at school. The information that he was failing a course came as big, unwelcome news. She was angry at her son and concerned only about how this made her look. She assumed that because he's older, he can handle what comes up in his life and doesn't need any support. In fact, she needs him to support her by babysitting. The conversation dissolves into a fight, a threat, and lot of attitude from both of them.

The slow parent already knew what was happening in math before the teacher called. She and her son talked about it, and he devised a plan to improve his grade. With the clear evidence that the original plan isn't working, she supported his new idea, even though it meant hiring a babysitter. Because this new arrangement will cost her, the mother appropriately says she's going to check in regularly with her son. In the end, Jacob thanks his mom. They don't have a fight; they have a productive, respectful conversation.

When you and your teen have a sustainable, fun relationship, a bad grade in school isn't going to be a fight; it will be a conversation. Your teen won't try to hide the grade and will come to you with questions and ask for help or advice. But if you don't have a good relationship with your teen, the F may be the least of the things you don't know about and won't see coming.

Here's another set of fast parenting and slow parenting scenarios that emphasize the results of parenting every day, or not. The teen daughter is pregnant.

Sarah: Dad, I really need to talk to you.

Dad: Look, I'm kind of busy right now; can't this wait until the weekend?

Sarah: But I've been waiting to talk to you; I really need to do this now.

Dad: Okay, what?

Sarah: Dad, stop working on the computer and listen.

Dad: Fine ... there, are you happy? I've turned off the computer. What is it?

Sarah: I'm pregnant.

Dad: You are what!

Sarah: I'm pregnant, Dad.

Dad: You're only 16! How did this happen? Well, never
mind, I know how this happened! How far along
are you?

Sarah: Almost twelve weeks.

Dad: You're kidding?! The choices are narrowing pretty
fast. #@#@#%%##$$#!! Why didn't you tell me
sooner?

Sarah: I tried two or three times, and you kept telling
me you were too busy, we'd talk later, can't it wait
until the weekend, that you have to take this call,
that you're in the middle of a project. I figured
you would realize something was up when I kept
trying to talk to you. I can't believe you haven't
noticed I've been throwing up every morning.

Dad: I don't pay attention to what you do in the bathroom!

Sarah: Apparently not! What do you pay attention to?

Dad: Well, you've been more moody, lately. So I just left
you alone.

Sarah: Now you know why.

Dad: I hope you aren't expecting to bring a baby in this
house!

Sarah: Don't worry, Dad, I'll figure it out.

Here's the slow parenting version of the same conversation.

Sarah: Dad, I need to talk to you.

Dad: Okay sweetie, let me turn off the computer.

Sarah: Dad, I'm pregnant.

Dad: Honey, are you okay?

Sarah: No, I'm really scared. I don't know what to do.

Dad: How far along are you?

Sarah: Five or six weeks, I think.

Dad: Well, that gives us time to look at all the choices
and options. I'm really glad you told me. I noticed
you've gotten sick the last two mornings, and I
was going to ask you about it today.

Sarah: Oh, Dad, what I'm going to do?

Dad: When did you find out?

Sarah: I did a home pregnancy test yesterday. All I wanted to do was talk to you, but I had to tell my boyfriend first.

Dad: How is he?

Sarah: He's pretty scared and doesn't know what to do, either.

Dad: Okay, we need some accurate information, so let's go see the doctor to find out exactly how far along you are and hear about all your choices. I'll take tomorrow off from work, and we'll do this together.

Sarah: Thanks, Daddy.

In the fast parenting conversation, the dad gets the news at the last possible moment. The conversation is a crisis. Sarah tells her dad because she has no choice, and she doesn't expect to get any support. While she has tried numerous times to tell him, the dad's blinders keep him from noticing she needs to talk. Even though she forces the conversation to tell him she's pregnant, she is essentially left to her own devices.

In the slow parenting conversation, Sarah comes to her dad almost immediately, knowing she will get support. The pregnancy isn't a huge surprise because he has been paying attention, and he's immediately concerned for her emotionally and physically. No matter what the decision, their relationship is stronger.

Parenting every day works best when the other attitudes of slow parenting are in play. In fact, you need to parent every day to do the other attitudes. While this is the final attitude, it is essential to all the others. When you parent every day, you invite your teen into the relationship with you. Even if you're physically apart, with today's technology, you have many ways to make the offer and follow through.

EXERCISE
Ideas for Parenting Every Day

1. Literally invite your teenager to be in conversation with you at least one time every day for a month. You can invite him verbally, leave a voice message, text him, email him, tweet him, or send a Facebook message. You can leave a note on her door, on her car, in her lunch, or on the bathroom mirror. Get creative and make sure there's no repercussion if she says no. Just extend the invitation every day and watch what happens.

2. Ask your teenager what he needs from you today and then give it to him if you possibly can. If you can't, ask what else you can do.

3. Try four to six different things from this list of ideas for parenting every day and letting your teenager know she's special and you like her.
   - Create a ritual such as popping your head in his bedroom door before you go to sleep, asking how his day was or what he might need from you tomorrow.
   - Stop whatever you're doing when she accepts your invitation to interact.
   - Realize that not all teens need to talk to interact. Do something together.
   - Ask about his music; listen to a new favorite song.
   - Watch one of her TV shows with her, or even without her, and then later ask a question about it.
   - Ask about a project or assignment at school.
   - Attend an event he is part of.
   - Bring her a coffee while she's studying.
   - Take him for pizza after practice.
   - Help her do one of her chores during finals week.
   - Leave a small gift for him on his pillow.

4. Now add to this list in your journal; get creative with both your invitations and finding new ways to interact.

Chapter Nine

Limits and Punishments

"My mom definitely parents. I have rules and I get in trouble when I break them. The difference is that she almost never gets mad, and she doesn't make me feel bad about myself when I mess up."
—Margaret, age 18

*I*n *Slow Parenting Teens*, the setting of limits and punishments is thought out, deliberate, and builds your relationship. Limits and punishments are not snap reactions to crisis situations, nor are they unilateral decisions intended to manage your teen's behavior. Instead, they are opportunities for your teen to use the safe place you've created to build your relationship. Often the conversations are uncomfortable for you and your teen, and you both grow.

If the purpose of setting limits and punishments is not to manage your teen's behavior, then why do it? You create limits to manage your selfish fears. Whether you're a fast or slow parent, the purpose of limits and punishment is ultimately to maintain your own sense of emotional safety and manage the fears you have for yourself. We all do it. The difference between fast and slow parents is how you do it and whether or not you own it.

If you've come this far in the book, you know that all the reasons fast parents give for limits and punishments are motivated by selfish fears masquerading as noble fears. The idea that limits are for your teen's safety, his own good, his life education, his future ... well, we know those are covering your subconscious, selfish fears.

On a personal level, when you're in the mindset of a fast parent, why do you set limits and punishments? Often you believe if you don't punish your teen, you're agreeing with his choices and somehow giving permission for behavior you don't like. You honestly believe your teen is incapable of making good life decisions or daily choices, and that limits and punishments will teach useful life skills. You fear you aren't a good parent if you let any "bad" behavior slide. You fear your teen will take advantage of you if you aren't vigilant. He will grow up to be rude, manipulative, and selfish. You set limits and punishments to control his behavior, and when he crosses them, you punish him in an effort to correct him.

Does this work? Absolutely. You can control your teen's behavior with limits and punishments. You have the authority and power to be successful, but you'll pay a high price: your relationship.

To move toward slow parenting, you can learn how to set limits and punishments that actually build a relationship with your teen. Start by understanding that your rules have to do with *your* fears and needs, not your teen's needs. Sometimes the only way to handle your fears is by getting your teenager to behave differently, and this is fine. While setting limits and punishments, you can take ownership that they are for you. Your limits can deal with your selfish fear AND be in your kid's best interest, such as setting an early curfew before an exam. But as a slow parent, you understand that the curfew is first and foremost about your own fears.

Trying to convince your teen that a rule is for his own good is a set-up for a fight. Slow parents don't go there.

When slow parenting, you own that your limits and punishments are motivated by your needs and fears, and you're prepared to talk about them. You allow enough room for your teen to react, to push against the limits, to be frustrated, to negotiate, and to lash out. You've created a safe place for this purpose. Your teenager gets to have a response. Just remember to not take the reaction personally, or you can get re-hooked into fast parenting. You can empathize with her. No one likes having to live with boundaries set by others, but you don't have to alter your limit just because she's upset. Your teen's reaction may trigger even more of your fears, so own them, too. Both of you will grow in these intense interactions, and so will your relationship. The key is to never make the limits or punishment about what she needs or what is "best" for her.

Fear of other people's judgments can also re-hook you into fast parenting. You can fall prey to judgments when you're seen as too lenient, too accepting of your teen's reaction, or too permissive of his behavior. Your ex-husband thinks you're more concerned about your teen liking you than about being his parent; the teacher thinks you don't participate enough in his education; your in-laws don't like the way you let your son talk to you or other adults. These are real pressures on slow parents, so make room for them. Understand that you are, to some degree, affected by what other adults think of you, but keep the goal in mind. You're building a relationship with you teen. Not everyone will agree with the way you parent, even as they envy the relationship you have with your teenager.

To talk about punishment, let's start with a distinction between consequences and punishment. Consequences are the natural fallout of an action, good or bad. Punishments are manufactured. For fast parents, punishments are intended to manage a teen's behavior and often involve shame and fear.

These punishments do work; you can manage a teen's behavior with punishment, but to the detriment of your relationship. For slow parents, punishments are rare because slow parents tend to get out of the way of natural consequences and let them do the work. In slow parenting, punishments are used to emphasize a lesson when the natural consequences are too subtle or not immediate enough to make the point. Given a choice, though, slow parents choose the natural consequences every time.

When creating limits and punishments, we suggest a few ideas to consider.

a. Whatever you create, you have to enforce. Don't make yourself crazy.

b. Too many limits will eventually damage your relationship, even if you own them. Try to stick to just a few.

c. Whenever possible, stay out of the way of natural consequences; they are the best teachers.

d. If possible, make punishment clear in advance. That way your teen can decide if the punishment is worth stepping over the limit.

e. Wait until you are not angry to set a punishment.

f. Keep punishments to the point, matter of fact, and as free of your emotion as possible. Your teen will bring plenty of emotion for both of you.

g. Don't bluff. Ever. Bluffs are threats, and you lose credibility with them.

Setting limits and punishments is part of parenting. All aspects of parenting are opportunities to build a sustainable, fun, and respectful relationship with your teenager. Even the most difficult, unpleasant aspects of parenting teens can build the relationship you want if you use the five attitudes. In fact, you often do the most work on your relationship during the difficult and unpleasant situations. So welcome them.

Let us show you examples of how the five attitudes become part of limits and punishments. When you steward your teen, you know what punishment will be effective with her. When you respect her personality, you allow her time alone to process the new limit or you create space for her to talk about it, if that's what she needs. With this approach you'll have many opportunities to catch her doing it right. If she ultimately respects the limit or responds to a punishment with a good attitude, you can thank her. If she presents a well thought-out alternative, you can praise her problem-solving and thinking skills. Once you let her know your fear and why you're setting this limit, you've created the perfect time to listen to her reactions, feelings, and concerns. When you parent every day, you tend to catch behaviors sooner, when the corrections can be smaller and celebrations can be instant and more numerous.

The following dialogues contrast fast and slow parenting in disciplinary situations. The first situation involves a 17-year-old boy and a broken curfew:

Dad: Where the hell have you been? It's 12:30 and you were supposed to be in at midnight. I didn't get a call or a text. I've been sitting here worrying. You are so disrespectful, and if you think you're going to put me through this and not get in trouble, you're out of your mind. Where were you?

Marcus: My phone died and I didn't know what time it was. I was with my friends. I knew I was a little late, but I figured you were already asleep and it wouldn't be a big deal. Sorry.

Dad: Really? Let me see your phone.

Marcus: Fine, here it is.

Dad: Next time you go out, you need to make sure your phone is charged. That was just irresponsible of you. And it isn't an excuse for being late, by the way.

Marcus: Okay, I'll make sure my phone is charged. Can I go to bed, now?

Dad: No, you're grounded. So I'm keeping the phone. Your curfew is now 11, and you are not going out this weekend.

Marcus: Fine. When do I get my phone back, and how long is my curfew 11?

Dad: Until you change that attitude, young man.

Marcus: That is completely unfair. You're so over-reacting to this.

Dad: Keep talking and I'll take away the car!

Marcus: So that means you'll be taking me to school and picking me up after practice at 4:30?

Dad: Okay, I won't take your car away, but if you don't change your attitude, things are going to get really ugly for you around here.

Marcus: So what's new?

Here is a slow parenting version of the same situation:

Dad: Marcus, where have you been? It's 12:30 and your curfew is midnight.

Marcus: I'm sorry Dad, my phone died. I knew I was a little late, but I figured you'd be asleep and it wouldn't be a big deal.

Dad: Well kiddo, tonight it was a big deal. I wasn't able to sleep because I was worried, and I have a big meeting tomorrow. So you know what to do.

Marcus: Okay Dad, I'm sorry. Here's my phone. When do I get it back?

Dad: Day after tomorrow. Would you like me to charge it for you?

Marcus: Yeah, thanks. I hope your meeting goes well. Good night.

Dad: Love you, son.

Yes, punishment *can* be that easy when you don't take it personally, you keep your emotions out of the punishment, and you don't make it about your teenager. These conversations occurred for the same reason, and both result in punishment for breaking a rule. And there the similarities end. The fast dad loads the conversation with all his anger, suspicion, and fear. He makes breaking this limit a personal attack by Marcus, and Dad attacks back to save face. Because Dad has more authority and Marcus has more pride, the interaction quickly spirals into a power struggle. The conflict is unnecessary, and the relationship is damaged.

In the slow parenting conversation, the dad and teen have already worked out the punishment for such an infraction. Dad doesn't question Marcus' story, and he doesn't take Marcus' lateness personally. The interaction is matter of fact and doesn't escalate into a power struggle or even a conflict. The conversation is almost pleasant. This may seem too easy. It may seem unrealistic to think Marcus doesn't fight back or blow up. However, this is realistic when you don't take it personally, have prearranged punishments, and when you keep the punishment simple and short. Both Marcus and his dad can live with Marcus not having a phone for a few days. Marcus feels the sting of the punishment, but the pain isn't bad enough to create resentment. The fast parent uses shame, punishment, threats, and his authority in an attempt to control Marcus' behavior and attitude. The slow parent uses a manageable, pre-arranged punishment to make his point. The slow parent is building toward a sustainable, respectful, and fun relationship in the future; the fast parent is condemning his future to more of the same.

Here's another example of slow parenting versus fast parenting discipline. This situation involves a prank gone bad. First, the fast parenting example:

Knock, knock.

Police Officer: Mrs. Cooper? Is this your daughter, Leanne?

Mom: Yes, that's my daughter.

Police Officer: Well, ma'am, she and some friends were caught egging a car, and unfortunately the car was badly scratched during the prank. The owner saw the kids and is pressing charges for vandalism. Here's a copy of her ticket, and you'll be getting more information from the courts.

Mom: What do you have to say for yourself, young lady?

Leanne: We really didn't mean to scratch the car. That was an accident.

Police Officer: Well, ma'am, your daughter is home safely. I'll be leaving.

Mom: Leanne, get in this house, NOW! You are only 13 years old, and already you're being brought home by the police for the whole neighborhood to see. What were you thinking?

Leanne: I'm really sorry. We thought it wasn't a big deal to egg a car. When the owner started yelling, we just grabbed our stuff to run away. I'm not sure exactly what happened or how the car got scratched; maybe it was Jackie's backpack with all her stuff hanging from it. It was an accident.

Mom: It was an accident that's going to cost you. You kids are going to have to pay to repair the car. If we have any fees or court costs, those are yours, too, young lady. You'll have to use the money you saved for your French trip. No French trip for you. And you will definitely be apologizing to the owners and washing their car. I am so embarrassed; I won't be able to hold my head up around Jackie's mother. I'll have to go with you to apologize and further embarrass myself. And now I can't trust you. Nice work. I hope you're happy because you are not leaving this house until school is out.

Leanne: I didn't mean to do anything wrong, Mom. What about Anna's birthday party on Saturday? I already have her present.

Mom: Tough, should have thought of that before you made the stupid decision to egg a car.

Leanne: Sorry, Mom. (She starts to cry.)

Mom: Tears aren't going to help. Just go to your room.

Here is the slow parenting version of the same situation:

Knock, knock.

Police Officer: Mrs. Cooper? Is this your daughter, Leanne?

Mom: Yes, that's my daughter.

Police Officer: Well, ma'am, she and some friends were caught egging a car and unfortunately, the car was badly scratched during the prank. The owner saw the kids and is pressing charges for vandalism. Here's a copy of her ticket, and you'll be getting more information from the courts.

Mom: Thank you, Officer. Come in, sweetie. Honey, you look upset. Do you need a hug?

Leanne: Yes. (She starts to cry.)

Mom: Come sit down and tell me what happened.

Leanne: Oh, Mom, everything got out of hand. We just thought it would be funny to egg Jackie's neighbor's car. We figured it would wash right off and wasn't a big deal. But then she saw us and starting yelling. We grabbed our stuff, and I think that's when Jackie's backpack scratched the car. We ran to Jackie's house, and a little while later the police knocked on the door. One officer stayed to talk to Jackie's mom and the other brought me here.

Mom: Wow, honey. Bummer. You know this is going to have consequences.

Leanne: Yeah, I know. How much do you think this is going to cost?

Mom: Well, it will probably be hundreds of dollars by the time it's done.

Leanne: Am I am going to have to pay for all of that?

Mom: Yes, sweetie, you are.

Leanne: But we didn't mean to cause the damage. That was an accident.

Mom: Yes, but just because it was an accident doesn't mean you don't have to accept responsibility for egging the car in the first place.

Leanne: But the only money I have is what I've saved for the French class trip this summer.

Mom: You have to take care of this first.

Leanne: But that means I won't get to go on the trip.

Mom: Yes, that's probably true.

Leanne: (Starts to cry again.) That doesn't seem fair, but I understand. Thanks Mommy, I am really sorry.

Mom: I know you are sweetheart, and I'm pretty sure you won't do something like this again.

Leanne: No way!

The fast parent takes Leanne's mistake and turns it into an intentional, personal, destructive act. She proceeds to shame her daughter in front of the police officer, point out the consequences, and add more punishments. Mom makes the situation about her own embarrassment and how Leanne is going to pay. There is no apparent concern for Leanne's feelings. Because Leanne tends to be quiet and passive, she doesn't fight back and keeps her feelings hidden. Their relationship is at risk.

The slow parenting version shows that sometimes the punishment comes from natural consequences and those consequences aren't easy for the parent or for the teenager. The slow parenting mom doesn't need to pile on consequences or further shame Leanne by pointing out her bad judgment. From stewarding her teen, she knows Leanne understands she made a mistake. Because Mom respects Leanne's quiet personality, she asks Leanne to talk about her feelings, and then listens without correcting or judging her. Mom doesn't rescue Leanne from the consequences of her choices, but she does provide comfort. This tough situation is strengthening their relationship.

——◆ ◆ ◆——

Everything that happens between you and your teenagers can either strengthen or damage your relationship, depending on your reaction as the parent. You get to choose. That's why we say that if you don't have the relationship you want with your teen, you can change it—but you're the one who needs to change. You're the grown up, so take responsibility for your own fears, create a safe place for your teen, and use the five attitudes as guides for being a slow parent.

We can't tell you exactly what to do in particular situations. We don't know you or your teen, and we can't predict what you need to feel comfortable or what your teen needs each day to grow. But we know that if you want a sustainable, fun, and respectful relationship, then moving toward slow parenting will get you there. You will stumble, and your teen will occasionally flip out. You both are human, but when you have a slow parenting relationship, you'll be able to apologize, accept an apology, and work together to strengthen your bonds. With a strong relationship, you can handle whatever situation comes up without having to risk estrangement. You can grow together and deeply enjoy the company of your teen now and through the future. All you have to change is you.

Chapter Ten

Slowing Down

> *"Even though my son is only 12, I learned that communicating my fears to him now is important."*
> —Nancy D., Colorado Springs

*N*o doubt you've noticed big differences between the fast parenting and slow parenting dialogues at the end of our chapters. The fast parents are a little harsh, and those slow parents seem a bit unreal. Don't they ever get upset? You probably thought, "That's not realistic, especially for my kid. And is it really so bad to be strict and make rules? They're still kids and they don't always make the best decisions when left to themselves." Perhaps it seems impossible for you to have these kinds of exchanges, but all the dialogues are based on real conversations. Trust the idea of slow parenting; it isn't so far beyond your reach.

Remember in Chapter Two when you tracked your own parenting style on the continuum between fast and slow parenting? Where did you land? You probably aren't as slow as you wish you were, meaning you don't yet have the relationship you want with your teenager. The promises of Slow Parenting Teens are that you *can* slow down and you *can* have those loving conversations, in time. The slow parenting dialogues you read are the results of persistent slow parenting. Slowing down takes time and attention, and you'll find that progress doesn't always move in a smooth, straight line. Give yourself a break and be patient.

As we watch parents slow down, we notice common issues that crop up for everyone. First, parents have a hard time identifying and owning their own selfish fears. That means their unacknowledged fears continue to be the prime motivators of their parenting decisions. Slow parenting requires substantial self-reflection, and sometimes it takes a while for parents to get the hang of separating their noble fears from their selfish ones. Parents like their justifications and noble fears. It does seem more acceptable to demand your teen dress a certain way because he'll never find employment with his low-slung pants than to realize you're selfishly afraid he'll drive you crazy if he doesn't get a summer job. Your noble fear seems like a much more valid reason to ask for a dress code change than the selfish fear of being irritated by your son.

If you really want to slow down, then ask yourself, "So what?" every time you find yourself on the verge of jumping into fast, reactive parenting. Usually, the answer isn't all that scary once you identify the fear. Then you can more easily step out of the way and let your teen make her own choices or allow natural consequences to guide her behavior. If the answer to "So what?" *still* scares you, then talk with another adult about your fear or set a limit with your teen. Your job is to lessen the chances that you'll jump in and start directing the scene for her. You can't build a positive, sustainable relationship if you're dictating all the shots. Talk about your selfish fears until you have an understanding of them, so they don't leap out of your mouth and become your teenager's problem, too.

You might also work on your sense of humor—especially the ability to laugh at yourself. You're trying to change a long-standing habit; give yourself time. The transition will be easier if you can laugh at your missteps and quickly move to what you'd like to try next time. You can use slow parenting attitudes with yourself as you slow down. Respect your own personality, listen to yourself, and catch yourself doing it right. Celebrate when you don't pick a fight; when you listen longer than you ever thought possible; when you trust his intuition; when you set a limit to protect yourself, not to manage your daughter; when you laugh with your sullen son, or have a long walk with your isolating daughter. Enjoy the changes and surprises.

We find parents enjoy telling us about their slow parenting "Aha!" moments. Here's an example from a parent who is actively and deliberately slowing down: Louisa has had a hard time with her 15-year-old daughter, Paige. They had a habit of getting into arguments when they needed to plan something or meet a deadline, especially regarding Paige's schedule. Paige is a busy girl, so they had a long record of low-level conflicts, and they were often grumpy with each other. This day brought a perfect set-up for a fight. Paige was traveling out of town with her school orchestra; she had a concert near home first, and then had a major project due at school immediately after returning home from the orchestra's road trip. Louisa proudly shared that she looked at the open, empty suitcase on Paige's bed and the books splayed on her desk and simply asked, "How can I help?"

This was so different for her she could hardly believe it, so she started laughing. In the past, Louisa would have looked at the mess and started bossing Paige around. Louisa's stress level would have gone off the scale over needing her daughter to have everything ready and in perfect condition. She feared she would look bad as a mom if Paige had anything amiss. Paige, of course, resented being told how to pack and prepare for her trip; she was in high school, old enough to pack for herself. They would have had a fight, for sure. *But not this time.* Louisa saw the set-up, felt her fears, owned them, and put them aside. Louisa was overjoyed, because together they figured out what needed to be done, and she got to see how Paige approached packing and planning for her upcoming events. Louisa is learning to slow down. Her success in this slow parenting moment will lead to other victories.

Another issue parents face as they begin to slow parent is the subtleness of the changes. In the example of Louisa and Paige, nothing dramatic happened. They didn't fight; they were a little more pleasant to each other. Packing for Paige's trip wasn't a big deal. As Louisa continues to practice the attitudes of slow parenting, their relationship will grow, and the drama will lessen. Some parents discount small changes because they think their relationship should have always been like this. You may think that removing the drama is just moving to normal; it isn't a huge change. When you start getting along better with your teen, you may not realize *it's progress.*

We suggest you give yourself structure for slowing down and allow yourself to recognize the changes. Try a 30-day plan. Set a few reasonable goals for your relationship and don't give up until the 30 days have passed. Maybe you want to work on parenting every day, so you establish a daily time to talk with your daughter. Honestly assess how many times a week you and your daughter currently have a real conversation that isn't about chores, homework, or some other transaction. Then for 30 days, invite your daughter to spend additional time with you. You can offer to go out for a treat, go for a walk, drive her somewhere, or simply ask her how her day went. Just offer the invitation to interact every day for 30 days. As you continue to make the offer, you'll learn what works and what doesn't. Don't take your daughter's reactions personally. She will accept some of your invitations and not others; it's not about you. Vary your approach, try something silly, and stretch toward your teen for 30 days.

At the end of the trial period, determine if you've made any progress in parenting every day.

♦ How often in the last week did you and your daughter have a good talk, with no arguing, no correcting, and where she actually shared?

♦ At the beginning, we told you that if you want a better relationship, you're the one who'll have to change. How have you changed during this trial period?

♦ What is working for you?

♦ What do you want to repeat?

♦ What will you remember not to try again?

♦ What do you notice about how you now relate to your daughter?

♦ Do you know more about what she's doing and how she thinks?

♦ Do you feel more connected, or not?

♦ Is she talking to you more often now than 30 days ago?

♦ What do you want to try next to get better at parenting every day?

Then pick another attitude and make your next 30-day plan. By making clear, specific plans you track and commit to, you'll be more alert to the positive changes that occur in you and in your relationship.

We've also noticed that teens don't always appreciate it when parents change, even if the change is for the better. They are wary. If you've been parenting one way up until now, it will be hard for them to believe any change is to be trusted. Your teenager will test your new limits, and you will not yet be secure in your new behaviors. Things are likely to get messy. You and your teen have adjustments to make. So when you first try slowing down, you may not get much applause from your children, and that can be disappointing. Please remember not to take personally your teens' reactions to anything, especially you. Stick with your 30-day plan and keep at it, noticing not only changes in your relationship with your kid, but also in yourself. Just because you change how you behave doesn't mean your teen will behave differently or appreciate what you're doing. You're the grown up; you're the one who can understand the long view. Don't give up just because your son storms out of the room. What do you expect when you change the rules of the game?

If you're disappointed, talk to another adult about how you feel and what you're trying to achieve. Perhaps you'll inspire this other adult to also try slow parenting; maybe you'll just vent enough to clear your mind and remind yourself why you're working so hard. But whatever you do, don't make your hurt feelings your teen's problem. Be patient and persistent if you want your teenager to trust your changes.

Another choice for handling your disappointment is to create feedback loops. With regular feedback about how you're doing, you can develop reasonable expectations of your relationship with your teen. Ask your partner or spouse for observations about your interactions with your adolescent. If your partner is also trying to slow down, you'll have terrific conversations! But even if it's just you slowing down, you can ask for perspective on how you and your teen are getting along. You can also tell your teenager what you're doing and why you're doing it. He may be very supportive of having a better relationship. Ask him for feedback on your efforts and ask for suggestions about what you could do differently. You will learn about him, too, so that you can better steward him moving forward. The feedback may feel negative, but we believe with direct feedback, you'll gain the information you need to keep moving toward a fun and sustainable relationship.

As you slow down, remain open and curious about your teen. A new relationship will start to form, and you don't want to miss a thing. Also, your teen will continue changing, and the closer you become, the more she'll share with you. Not only is your relationship evolving, but so is the person on the other side of it. If you remain open and curious, you'll have a chance to appreciate any move your teen makes toward you. You'll catch the gentle request that you be present for an event. You'll notice she turns off her phone when she comes to the dinner table without being asked or reminded. You'll be alert to changes in her attitudes and opinions. And when she tells you about some idea she finds new and cool, you'll be able to genuinely respond, "Tell me more," even if you already know all about that subject. By staying open and curious, you will build a safe place for your teenager to be exactly who she is; a place where she won't be judged or corrected. Now *that* is slow parenting.

In another real life example of slowing down, Gerald described a potentially difficult time with his 17-year-old daughter, Anna. She has always enjoyed performing in theater and can be a drama queen in her own life as well. Their old dog had grown suddenly ill and was dying. Gerald shares custody of his children with his ex-wife, and they all loved the dog, so he arranged for everyone to get together. Gerald and his ex-wife agreed they should all say good bye to the dog and have her euthanized. That's when Anna started crying and struggling out loud and all over the house about whether or not she wanted to be present when the dog died. She went on for quite a while. Gerald was proud to report that he remembered this is Anna's personality. She is dramatic. It made it easier for him to step back and just listen to Anna as she talked her way through her decision. He didn't try to correct her, affect her decision, or get her to choose more quickly. In the end, she decided to stay with the dog and cried through the whole thing.

"It was amazing to me," he said. "I didn't get agitated. I just held the space for her to decide. I even think it went faster than if I'd told her to behave more calmly. I know we would have had a fight. But no. We just said goodbye to the dog and held each other." Anna probably didn't notice her father had changed, but she gained a positive memory of her divorced family at a trying time. That made Gerald's efforts worthwhile.

Beth told us about how she found "tag team" parenting. Twelve-year-old Zach spent the afternoon whining about his homework and then sketching a face—which was not part of his homework. Beth was seething at his lack of progress, and Zach watched her out of the corner of his eye, still sketching. When Beth's husband walked in, she was scolding Zach for not getting down to work, and Zach was becoming defensive. She realized she was only going to escalate the situation and that she needed to get away and cool down. She looked at her husband and son and said, "I bet Dad can be more helpful; I'm going to garden for a while." Immediately Dad sat and listened to Zach whine, and then they began organizing his papers. Beth was enormously relieved that she noticed her own tension building and chose to unplug from it. She took care of herself and avoided further damage to her relationship with her son.

Slowing down is about progress, not perfection. We know there will be bad days and tension-filled moments. Things will be said and mistakes will happen, but when you're earnestly working for a slow parenting relationship, forgiveness comes easier. You can forgive yourself faster, and you will apologize with no loss of face. Eventually, so will your teen.

Chapter Eleven

Slow Parenting in a
Variety of Family Configurations

*"My wife and I saw each other as saboteurs in our parenting
efforts. Now, we want to be more supportive and not
take each other's comments personally!"*
—David N., Colorado Springs

Slow parenting can be used in a wide of range of family
configurations that exist in our society. If you're a divorced
parent, a single parent, a grandparent raising a grandchild,
a blended family of step-children and step-parents, part of a
multigenerational family all living together, or in a nuclear
family where one parent is and one parent is not trying to
be a slow parent, you can *always* work on your relationship
with your teen. Each of these family configurations have
more than one adult who's important to your teenager. Even
if you're a single parent, your child has other important
adults in his life, and you have to talk to these other adults,
whether you want to or not. Remembering the five attitudes
of slow parenting can help you create a sustainable, fun, and

respectful relationship with your teen no matter the setting. The five attitudes will also help you negotiate the complex terrain of parenting with other adults.

Raising your child with other adults can be confusing for you and for your teenager. As always with slow parenting, we ask you to identify and acknowledge your fears and keep them out of your relationship with your teen. She has enough to deal with on her own; she doesn't need your fears as well. Work to discern your noble and selfish fears about having other adults in your teenager's life, especially those who aren't interested in the idea of slow parenting. Talk with a like-minded adult about your fear and be alert to how your fears influence your parenting decisions.

For example, you nobly fear creating chaos for your teenagers, so you decide to go along with the other parent's punishments, even when you disagree. But what motivates your decision is the selfish fear of having a fight with the other parent. Fear about what others think of your parenting can quickly show up in complex family arrangements. You may fear being judged as too much of a friend and not enough of a parent because of your slow parenting relationship with your teen. This fear may cause you to treat your teen differently when you're with others than when you're alone with him. Acknowledging fears will help you be a consistent slow parent, no matter what the other adults in your teenager's life are doing.

The fundamentals of slow parenting don't change, no matter what the family configuration. Your relationship with your teen is yours. You may have others watching and commenting, but what goes on between you and your child is up to you. You can use the five attitudes in your interactions with your teen, even when other parents don't have a slow parenting relationship with the same kid.

There will always be adults in your teen's life who don't agree with slow parenting; this challenge remains constant. You may be in a nuclear family where everyone is on the same page of this slow parenting book, but some significant people in your teenager's life will not be interested in these ideas. If it isn't other parents and family members, it may be coaches, teachers, mentors, and ministers who have different ideas about what motivates teenagers—ideas that clash with the attitudes of slow parenting. You'll have to work out agreements with these valuable people, and you'll need to accept their ideas as, hopefully, they learn to value yours.

Your teen is the best commonality in your complex family constellation. Your teen is adaptable and will be able to shift from relationship to relationship. The differences among important adults will give your son plenty to think about and discuss with you. He'll have terrific opportunities to experience how he responds to the different ways adults have of correcting, motivating, and relating to him. With you as a sounding board, he can learn a great deal about himself.

Not only do the fundamentals of slow parenting stay the same with changing family arrangements and dynamics, so do the five attitudes. You can apply the first attitude, stewarding your teenagers, by using your time together to get to know your ever-changing and growing son or daughter and to nurture the interests and ideas that are taking shape. You may feel overwhelmed with step children, out of date with your grandchildren, or limited in your time with your children, but when you parent with curiosity and without judgment, you can guide and nurture the teens in your life.

The second attitude also remains the same: respect their personalities. The other adults in your teen's life will have opinions about her personality and needs, but you must form your own. Take time to create opportunities and watch her in many settings. Treat your teen as the unique person she is and remember there is no cookie-cutter approach to all adolescents. Even if your daughter's wardrobe or your son's choice of girlfriend makes you a little nervous, own your fears and stay in relationship with them.

Catch Them Doing It Right, the third attitude, may need a little fine-tuning. We always support complimenting your teens instead of correcting them. Catching them doing it right will help you create that vital safe place for your teen to talk with you. If what you're praising is considered a bad thing by the other adults in the room, wait until you're in private to compliment your teen. By doing so, you can easily avoid setting your kid up for criticism from adults in his life or witnessing a disagreement between you and another adult. Nevertheless, always look to catch your teen doing it right.

Listening is another slow parenting attitude that requires extra thought when you're working in a complex family arrangement. As we've already pointed out, listening without interrupting or redirecting your teenager is a skill that requires practice. The practice is worth every minute because you'll be on your way to creating a solid, trusting relationship. If you only have partial contact with your teen, then you should be careful not to be judgmental or critical when he talks about the other environments in which he lives. Use most of your time with him listening.

Listen to your teen until she finishes talking. Don't join in if she's complaining about the other adults. If she complains, listen but don't take sides. Ask if she has more to say. Listen for what she's learning and watch for how she reacts. When she's finished, you can ask her what she thinks she should do next. And then listen some more. Just as your relationship with your daughter is between her and you, her relationship with other adults is between her and them. We encourage you to keep your feelings, especially anger, out of the conversation.

Finally, we encourage you to parent every day. With texting, email, cell phones, Facebook and Skype, you have myriad ways to touch base with your children, even if you don't see them every day. Being part of your teen's life every day is part of how you create a fun, sustainable relationship. No matter how many other people are parenting your teenager, make yourself available. Don't pass up the chance to know what's going on and what your son or daughter is thinking.

We want to point out a few traps for parents in a complex family situation, and we think these apply even if you aren't trying to slow parent. The first trap is competing with the other adults in some way. You might be trying to plan the coolest vacation, have your teenager like you better, do the most fun stuff, or just spend more money. This competition has little to do with developing a fun, respectful, and sustainable relationship with your teenager, but it has everything to do with you and your fears. It seems a great waste of the time you have with your teenager to question him about what other adults are doing. If you find yourself comparing yourself to the other adults in your kid's life and trying to compete with them, it's time to dig deeper, find out what you're afraid of, and keep that fear out of your relationship with your teen.

Another trap you can fall into is trying to avoid all conflict with your teen. You can't have a sustainable relationship and avoid all conflict. Parenting, especially slow parenting, requires you to lay down limits and allow consequences. In an effort to avoid conflict, you might keep your distance and miss out on stewarding your teen or getting to know her personality because you're afraid of what you'll find. In your quest to avoid conflict, you might choose not to have difficult conversations that will grow your relationship, and you might choose not to invite your teen daily to have a talk. We think this trap is about your fear: fear of losing contact with your children, fear of being judged by others, or fear of not being the "fun" parent (there's that competition again). We urge you to have an honest relationship with your teen— conflicts and all. We know relationships get stronger when they grow through tough times as well as good times.

A final trap for parents in complicated family arrangements is being hypersensitive to judgment, especially if you feel isolated as a parent. If you're the only one who is slow parenting, you can easily get tunnel vision about how your teen should be parented. Comments from others about how you handle your children and what you do and don't do may feel like poisoned darts. Such sensitivity leads you to react harshly to other adults. Instead of nursing hurt feelings, we encourage you to look at what you're afraid of from these comments. Then find other people who are interested in slow parenting. Share with them and compare notes. Gain perspective and step away from other people's judgments.

This is where using the attitudes of slow parenting can be useful with adults. If you find yourself wanting to comment on or change how someone else is interacting with your teenager, ask yourself what you fear. Ask, "So what if another adult parents differently?" Reflect on this until you know how it does affect you, and you'll find that you have more options about how to go forward with that adult. For example, if you wish your co-parent would stop telling your son he has to go to a particular college, ask yourself why you care so much. You might have the noble fear that your son is feeling pressured, but if you push a little harder, you may find less noble fears. Maybe you think that college is too expensive. You might find that you're tired of your time with your son being taken over by rehashing arguments with his other parent. Now you can address your selfish fears about money, or you can figure out how to get out of the middle of their fight. Either way, you have options that involve only you instead of trying to change someone else.

When you're talking with the other adults in your teenager's life, respect their personalities just as you respect your teen's personality. Put your fears aside and pay attention to how they see the world and relate to this shared responsibility: your child. You may not want to be best friends, but you do need to establish a working relationship. When you respect their personalities, you'll learn how they work through issues; you can be patient and avoid putting energy toward trying to change them. Instead, put that energy into building the relationship with your teenager.

You can also catch the other adults doing it right. Thank your adult daughter for being reliable and getting your grandchildren's schedules coordinated. You can thank your ex-wife's new partner for asking to talk to you in private instead of in front of your son. Without being patronizing, you can show your appreciation when other adults accept that you have different limits and punishments at your house. You can thank the coach or teacher for not criticizing you. Once you start looking for opportunities to say thank you, your attitude toward all the other adults may shift, reducing the amount of friction in your life and your teenager's life.

You can practice listening to your co-parents, too. Listen with curiosity about their perspectives, expectations, and concerns. Celebrate with them the pleasure of being in your teen's life. Listen to try to understand their perspective, knowing that understanding it doesn't mean you agree with it. You may have a situation where another adult insists you set limits and punishments the same way he does with your teenager. This might happen in a nuclear family where one parent is slow parenting and the other isn't. By listening well, you can understand the other person's point of view and thought process, but not have to agree. We do advise you to be aware of selfish fears that are coming up for you regarding this disagreement. Being aware of your own feelings helps you be proactive, not reactive. If you recognize your fears, you have a much greater chance of finding a way forward without a fight or damage to your relationship with your teenager.

Parent every day is the final slow parenting attitude. When applied to the adults in your teen's life, it means you invite the other parents to discuss your teen with you. Shutting out the others won't help the relationship with your teen or make it easier to navigate a complex family situation. We urge you to extend an invitation to talk and set aside any adult conflicts between you, so that all the grown-ups support your teen. We also encourage you to accept similar invitations from the other adults to support your teenager.

Complex family situations provide many opportunities to role model for your teen about how to work with others who have differing perspectives and goals. You can be an example of how to disagree without criticism or letting the situation disintegrate into fights and power struggles. You can interact with adults with whom you disagree in a way that is respectful and considerate. You can show your teen that you can put aside your opinions for her sake and the sake of your relationship with her. You can even use differences between adults to discuss slow parenting with your teen and why you practice it. The attitudes of slow parenting, when practiced in the entire family constellation, will surprise you with the many ways they strengthen your relationship with your teenager.

Chapter Twelve

Slow Parenting More Than One Teen

"Kids spell love T-I-M-E."
—John Crudele

*M*any families have more than one child in the teenage years at the same time, especially when we consider those years to span from age 12 until 22. If you have more than one child, you're probably raising two teens simultaneously. How do you apply the five attitudes separately to each one? Is it fair to treat one differently from the other? Is it right to have different punishments for each kid? How does it work when you're trying to listen effectively to more than one kid on the same day? What if your teens have opposite personalities? How do you avoid getting lost in the logistics of life and stay focused on building relationships? How do you have a private relationship with each of your teens? These are great questions, and if you're even asking them, you can be assured you're moving toward slow. Parenting multiple teens does have its own challenges.

First let's discuss a few myths around parenting multiple children. One common belief is that you should be fair and equitable to all your children. Somehow, you think being completely even handed is a positive reflection of how well you're doing as a parent. You measure yourself by how evenly you divide your time, money, resources, and attention.

In this setting, fair and equitable are set ups for frustration and failure. No one-size-fits-all exists when it comes to parenting teens. You have set an impossible standard for yourself. What's worse, your teenagers will resent you because this standard ignores their individuality and causes them to constantly compare and look for inequities. They may use it against you. Instead of working together to find a fun and creative path forward, you and your teens get into disputes about the past where you defend your parenting and your kids feel unfairly treated. In terms of creating a sustainable relationship with all your teenagers, trying to be fair and equitable leads to disaster.

Another myth of parenting multiple teens is that you can find a magic wand to make *everyone* happy. You believe if you're resourceful and logical enough, you'll discover a fantastic solution and explain it well enough so all the kids, the other adults, and the extended family will be in agreement. You count on your teens to understand the larger context and accept your solution as the best possible way to move forward, and you count on the other adults to agree with your logic. This myth has the corollary that you can parent so no one is mad at you or anyone else. As they say, "How has that been working for you?"

The desire for universal, family agreement comes from a fear that's common to all parents with more than one child. In its noble version, you fear one or more of your children will be upset, hurt, disappointed, or feel rejected. Your selfish fear is that your teenagers will blame you for the fight. We urge you to recognize that when you try to please everyone, you cannot possibly succeed. With multiple teens, someone is likely to be mad at you at least once in a while; that's normal and unavoidable. If you're parenting to avoid a teenager's anger, then you're fast parenting from fear.

Another myth is that if you parent correctly, your children will all be close friends. You believe that on the strength of having been raised by you, your teens will love each other and be favorite companions. While it's reasonable to think your teens will acknowledge one another and hopefully look out for each other, it isn't reasonable to believe these diverse people will have a close relationship. Your noble fears may be that they won't have a support system in their lives; they'll end up alone and separate from the family. The selfish fear may be that you'll look bad because your family isn't close, and this will be a hassle for you at future family gatherings. If your children aren't close, it will be hard to get them all around the table for that perfect holiday meal you fantasize about.

We all fall prey to these images of perfect families, but that's all they are: images. In the real world, families experience stress and difficulties no matter how you parent your children. Focusing on the images of a perfect, peaceful family is like focusing on your teens' behavior. By now, you know slow parents don't measure the success of their parenting by how their children turn out; they measure their success by the relationship they have with their children. Do your best to focus on your relationship with each of your children, not on how the whole gang gets along.

These myths and images take us back to Chapter 3 and knowing your own fears as you make parenting decisions. You bring to your current family the fears and beliefs of the family you were raised in, as well as the anxieties generated by our culture. If you were the youngest child, you may be especially sensitive to any pressure you see your older children place on your youngest. If you were the odd one out in your family, you may be touchy about any teasing endured by your teen with unusual interests. If you were an only child, you might be shocked by how siblings interact. Reflect on which of your buttons get pushed when your children work out their relationships. Know and handle your fear the best you can, so you can slow parent *all* your teens at the same time, minus the overlay of subconscious fears.

Now you're ready to bring the five attitudes of slow parenting into the family portrait: steward your teens, respect their personalities, and catch them doing it right while you listen and parent every day. When you steward your teens, you're paying individual attention to each of your children, so you have to release the idea of being fair and equitable. Your teens will have a wide range of interests, goals, needs, and strengths. When you treat them the same way, you ignore their individuality, which runs utterly counter to stewarding. Stewarding means you customize your parenting and create occasions for having a private relationship with each child. Your knowledge of each teen will help you handle them individually, but with the same motivation: to build a fun, respectful, and sustainable relationship.

Here's an example: Andrew has two sons. His older son Josh is similar to Andrew in temperament and interests. When Josh was 12, he wanted to play soccer for two seasons a year as well as run track and take piano lessons. He liked staying busy and loved the way his different activities made him feel. He took piano lessons before school so he could make track practice after school. Having full days made sense to him, and he still managed to finish his homework. He was an easy kid to talk with about his plans, and Andrew recognized himself in his older son. Josh knew his dad was willing to drive to out-of-town soccer games on weekends only if he took care of his equipment and was ready for each trip. Andrew understood this high energy, tightly scheduled life. He packed his younger son, Jimmy, into the car for trips to practices and games.

When Jimmy was 12, Andrew had to adjust. Jimmy wasn't organized or driven to excel in sports. He preferred watching TV after school and didn't enjoy competitive sports. He wanted to play music, but didn't want the structure of lessons, much less before school. Andrew wasn't sure this more laid back son would be as successful as his older brother. Andrew worried about Jimmy and sometimes pushed him to be more like his brother. But one day when he caught himself arguing with his younger son, he stopped in his tracks. He had to steward this kid, too. Andrew began to learn what made this teenager tick. He discovered that finding resources for his younger son was more helpful than planning his activities. He learned to ask questions about Jimmy's interests, even when he didn't understand them. Andrew stretched toward his younger son. In stewarding both teens, he learned to respect their personalities, even when one's personality was the opposite of his own.

Here's another example of how the second Slow Parenting Teens attitude, respecting their personalities, can help with parenting more than one teenager.

Cynthia's 15-year-old daughter accepts being sent to her room as a punishment for talking on the phone at dinner. When she returns downstairs to the rest of the family, she wants to talk about how she felt when she was sent to her room, what she thought about, and make sure no one is still mad.

Cynthia's 13-year-old daughter also accepts being sent to her room, but she prefers not to talk afterward. In fact, she said, "I've completed my punishment, why do I have to talk about it, too? Am I still being punished?" Two different daughters, two opposite reactions to the same situation. Is the punishment fair? Yes, if it stops with being sent to their rooms. Is the punishment equal and identical? Not if the younger daughter has to talk afterward, it isn't. Cynthia knows about her daughters' personalities from stewarding them, so she listens to the oldest process experiences out loud, but leaves her younger child alone to process on her own. Cynthia knows being fair doesn't always mean equal or identical. A reward for one teen could be a punishment for another. What is fair depends on their personalities.

The third attitude, catch them doing it right, can also guide you as you parent more than one teenager. In this case, you need to consider *what, how, when,* or *if* you should mention something. Here's what we mean: Let's say you have a 19-year-old and a 12-year-old. Their age difference means you catch them doing different things right. The 19-year-old left gas in the tank when she used your car. That's worth mentioning! The 12-year-old remembered to brush his teeth, also worthy of praise. You'll have to remember to catch the younger one doing things right even though you seemingly have bigger fish to fry with the older one.

From stewarding and respecting your children, you learn how praise feels to them. One teen might like an ice cream cone to celebrate, while the other just wants a hug. One wants you to say something at the dinner table; another will give you the death glare if you do; and the third appreciates a knowing smile and a nod. The same kind of praise has different effects, depending on how you steward each teen and based on her personality. If you're strongly extroverted or introverted, you may only be aware of how *you* like praise. To slow parent, you must extend yourself and learn what each of your teens thinks is praise. One size does not fit all.

The slow parenting teens attitudes take on special importance when you have several teenagers. We encourage you to steward, respect, and praise not only each child, but also their relationships with one another. You may have a picture in your mind of how your kids should get along, and that vision will be challenged. To be frank, your children's relationships with each other are their own, not yours. However, as the parent you can support their relationships by stewarding them, respecting their natures, and by catching them doing it right.

To steward your childrens' relationships, watch your children when they're together and listen to how they speak to each other. You won't see and hear everything, nor do we advocate that you try, but you can gain an understanding of how they work out their own relationship. Don't jump in at the first sign of a problem. They need time and space to work on their own relationship. The information you gain from observation may show you things to praise or discuss when you privately listen to each sibling.

You will definitely get a sense of what your kids are interested in doing together, and you should follow up on those opportunities. Perhaps they like to go to ball games or movies together. You can help them make arrangements. Perhaps they both want a piece of electronics; you can talk to them together about their plan, see what they've already figured out, and give them opportunities to earn money as a team. When you steward their relationship, you can guide them toward learning to respect each other's personalities.

Remember to respect the personality of each sibling relationship. While it may not be what you hoped for, it belongs to them, not you. They're working on it, and you get to measure how well you're parenting by your relationship with your teens, not by how they get along. To that end, respect their feelings about each other. Don't tell them how to feel. They may love each other, they may tolerate each other, and they may dislike each other; all in the same week. Remember not to take your teen personally, even when he says he doesn't like his sister. Their relationship will change, just as they do. You don't know how they should get along, so refrain from telling them what to do.

Many teens love their siblings and get along with them most of the time. Some teens just don't care for their brothers and sisters, and they don't have common interests or compatible personalities. Either way, you'll be stewarding each of them privately and you'll hear about it, especially if they're arguing. Fighting is often a big stressor for parents, and we know it's hard to be at your best when your children are in conflict. If you need to, talk with an adult to handle your own fears. Decide if you need to intervene in your children's argument. Just because you hear raised voice doesn't mean you must rush in stop them.

When you think you have to step in, separate the fighters. We encourage you to listen to each teen privately. Really listen.

Do not referee or take sides. You are Switzerland; be neutral. Show each kid how to respect the personality of the others involved. When you listen, you'll hear each kid complain about the others or "tattle" on them. This is privileged information. Consider what it will do to your relationship with your teen if you use this information against him or a sibling. If you feel compelled to act on the information, then you must talk to the informing teen first. When your teens ask for solutions and ideas, offer assistance but keep the focus on the kid in front of you. If necessary, set appropriate limits and punishments for each teenager, separately.

By watching their relationship grow and being on hand every day, you'll see the strengths of their bond and catch them doing it right. From stewarding them separately and together, you'll learn the most effective way of praising them. When you notice them enjoying each other, thank them. When you see them help each other out, thank them. When they do something positive for or with each other, comment on it. When they leave each other alone, notice. Trust them to figure out their relationship on their own terms. Step in rarely, and only after great discernment on your part.

All the while, maintain a private relationship with each of your teenagers, accepting each one and their relationship with one another. You cannot avoid having one or more of your children get angry with you or a sibling on occasion. But with a slow parenting relationship, you both know the conflict will resolve. You can maintain and build a strong relationship through these tough patches.

"Wow!" you're saying, "What a lot of time and energy!" Well, yes. It may seem easier to lay down the law for everyone in the house and demand obedience. If you do, you may even get the sort of behavior you want, but you won't have the relationships you want. Slow parenting is a kind of virtuous circle; each part contributes to the whole, building stronger relationships between you and all your teenagers, and it requires your time and focus.

Chapter Thirteen

Slow Parenting Teens
Who Have Big Problems

"Because our kid has big problems, we didn't know which of her behaviors were typical teenager behaviors and which were due to her diagnosis. Tonight I realized that her behaviors are the result of both, yet it doesn't matter! How we, her parents, respond rather than react is the bottom line."
—Tina N., Colorado Springs

We've talked a lot in this book about how to have a fun, sustainable relationship with your teenager. We've offered examples, tips, and dialogue to help you move toward slow parenting with your adolescent. We've shared the five attitudes that help you make the shift, and we've asked the big question, "What are you afraid of?" Now it's time to talk about teenagers and families who already face big problems and deal every day with their biggest fears, selfish and noble.

As an adolescent therapist, Marti has years of professional experience with troubled teens. Families never came to her because they wanted to improve the great relationship they already had. No, they came because their teenager was in serious trouble at school or with the law, was struggling with addictions or eating disorders, or the family had issues of grief and loss, divorce, death, or serious illness. The teen may have been diagnosed with attention deficit disorder or depression. There may have been suicide attempts, cutting, other self-harming behavior, or acts of violence toward others. There may have been autism or developmental issues, physical disabilities, learning disabilities, attachment disorder … and the list goes on. Families sought help because their relationships were eroding under the weight of these difficult issues.

Does Slow Parenting Teens work with these real, hardcore issues and problems? Can slow parenting help rebuild the relationships within a sorely troubled family, especially between the teen and parents? *Yes!*

For troubled teens, the basic concepts and five attitudes of Slow Parenting Teens do not change; what changes is how you measure your success as a parent. When you face severe behavioral problems, it's crucial that you do not equate your success as a parent with your teen's behavior. Please don't feed into the belief that you can parent your child out of her diagnosis, addiction, disability, depression, or bio-chemical issues. Your parenting didn't cause your teen's issues, and it can't remove them, either. But you can still have a sustainable and fun relationship with your adolescent.

Slow parenting teens is not about raising kids without problems, struggles, or even physiological challenges. It's about building and maintaining a relationship with your teen so you can move through the "trouble" together and not as enemies. You become your teenager's role model for owning tough feelings and choices. You demonstrate self-care, boundaries, and compassion.

We aren't saying that if you're a slow parent, your kid will avoid drugs or alcohol, won't need medication, will stop destructive behaviors, and will bring up her grades.

Slow Parenting Teens is not a cure for problems. But it does help you parent through the problems, so you can set strong boundaries and limits without becoming your teenager's enemy. Slow parenting is about building a relationship with your teenager, *not* managing behavior. That concept is difficult to remember when the teen's behavior is harmful to himself or others. When a teenager is hurting himself or someone else, the first order of business is to manage the situation so the damaging behavior stops, period. Notice, we said manage the *situation*, not the teenager.

We can't tell you how to handle every possible situation, so please get specific help for your family's challenges. However, we can tell you how to use slow parenting as one of your primary parenting tools. Even as you manage the crisis, you're still in a relationship with your teen. In fact, relationships often grow the most during these tough challenges. Your teenager will experience boundaries and limits from a loving parent who isn't spreading blame.

If you're concerned that your teenager may have a diagnosable issue, seek help from a therapist, family doctor, school counselor, or anyone who can accurately assess the problem and help you and your family find resources. We encourage you to use *Slow Parenting Teens* as one of your primary resources. The five attitudes and concepts work with all teens and the adults who care for them. These attitudes are effective because they help create and maintain a positive relationship between the adult and the teen. Such a relationship is essential when difficult issues are present.

The relationship between you and your teenager often succumbs to damage when big problems arise. Because the harmful situation must be controlled, it often feels as if the relationship with your teen is simply the price you must pay. No! Don't agree to pay that price. You can set limits, reinforce those limits, allow natural consequences, use the resource of medication, and even physically restrict your teenager while still building an intimate, supportive relationship. Not only *can* you build that relationship—you *must* build it in order to help yourself, your teen, and your family survive the challenges.

You will often be "the heavy," and your teen will often direct her frustration and pain onto you, which is why having a solid relationship foundation is critical. That's why asking yourself consistently "What am I afraid of?" is crucial. During these times, creating a safe place for your teenager is even more your job, and not taking her personally should become your daily, if not hourly, mantra.

Think about what you've learned so far in this book. Your job is to create a safe emotional place for your teenager to be a mess, explore options, be inconsistent, change her mind, let off steam, regroup, celebrate, be selfish, be generous, question himself, question you, express opinions, antagonize others, feel valuable no matter what, and push against boundaries. This is a place every teenager deserves and needs to maneuver through adolescence with all the chemical, physical, and neurological changes this developmental stage brings. Now add other brain or chemical changes, such as addictions, depression, situational challenges, grief and loss, or even learning challenges. These teens need that safe place even more. Because they may alienate people so easily, they are often left without a safe place to be loved for who they are.

This can be hard! When you're trying not to enable your teenager or when you're afraid of your teen harming herself or another person, it's easy to shut the door on the "emotional safe place" for her and just focus on managing the situation. New fears arise: *If I make it safe for her, will she take advantage of me and hurt herself again, or hurt someone else? If I let down my guard, will I have more of a mess to clean up later? Will other parents judge me since it may appear I'm condoning my kid's behavior by allowing her a place to vent and be inconsistent?*

Are you afraid of your teenager embarrassing you or afraid of a law suit against you because of your teen's choices?

These are selfish fears that can drive parenting decisions. The slow parenting process and the questions you ask are the same, whether your teenager is struggling with grades or addictions: "What am I afraid of for them? What am I afraid of for me? What limits and boundaries do I need to set to manage my fears? Have I owned my fears, or am I putting responsibility for my feelings onto my kid?"

When you're in the middle of severe issues, the consequences of your parenting decisions may seem bigger, more serious, and even life threatening, but the sequence of decision making is the same. Notice your own selfish fears. If a limit needs to be set, then set it, but admit that it's for your comfort, not your teen's best interest.

When you and your family are struggling with issues and challenges such as a mental health diagnosis, disabilities, addictions, or legal issues, creating the safe emotional place for your teen and acknowledging your fears are even more important. These two basic concepts of slow parenting make all the difference when your relationship is threatened by serious problems. Slow parenting also offers the five attitudes for relationship building. Let's look to see how those attitudes fit some of these challenging situations:

When your teen faces severe behavioral issues or emotional challenges, stewarding takes on more importance. Pay attention, notice, and be curious about your teenager. He is changing day to day, and sometimes hour to hour. His moods and attitude are information for you. His ability to express emotions and take responsibility for his choices tells you a lot about how he's progressing. Is he talking about his recovery group and sponsor, or does he avoid the conversation? Does he suddenly isolate in his room after a month of interacting with the family? Is he defensive more quickly than last week? Is he leaning into your hugs or pulling away? Notice, pay attention, and then check in with your adolescent. Do not assume you know what is going on—ask and pay attention!

When additional difficulties occur in the family, it's especially important to respect your teen's personality. Be careful not to diagnose your teen based on her appearance or current interests. Black clothes, eyeliner, and loud music don't necessarily mean she's depressed. Her low cut shirt and heavy makeup may *not* be telling you she has low self-esteem and is seeking male attention. Many teenagers explore styles, experiment with appearance, write dark poems, listen to music you probably won't like, and have a dependence on electronics you don't share. Respecting their personalities includes respecting their culture. Often when you face problems with your teen, it's hard to determine which behavior is part of their personality and which is a symptom of the problem.

Not every change in your teen is due to the problem he's facing. And even if the changes are related or symptomatic, the issue is now part of your teen's personality, based on the way we describe personality. A depressed adolescent may pay less attention to personal appearance, but pointing it out won't change the fact that he just doesn't feel like shaving. So respect the fact that he has a different standard of personal hygiene for now, and make sure to ask yourself, "What am I afraid of?"

Catching them doing it right can be hard when she's in legal trouble again, he's fighting at school for the second time this month, she's cutting herself again, and he's still lying and vandalizing cars. You're tired! You don't want to even appear to condone the destructive behavior. You do not agree with her choices, and you're exhausted from cleaning up yet another mess your teen made. We get it, really.

Catching them doing it right feels contrived when so many problems have piled up and so much of their behavior is "wrong." "You want me to catch him doing it right because he put away his shoes when he just hit his sibling in the face?" "You want me to thank her for finally putting the dishes away when it's the tenth time I've asked, and she told me to

*%#^ off the first nine times?" "You are seriously asking me
to thank him for sitting through a meal with the family when
he spent most of the dinner complaining about the food?"

Yes, that's exactly what we recommend. Slow parenting
is hard at times—especially when you have a teenager with
tough behavioral and emotional issues. But isn't that the kid
who most needs to be caught doing it right? He does so much
wrong in society's eyes and is so used to being labeled "the
screw up" that he may not remember how to catch himself
doing it right. Even as he pushes you away, notice anything
and everything he's doing well. This will help him stay
connected and help you see him not *as* the problem, but as
someone who's struggling with a problem.

Teenagers are developmentally self-absorbed. They're
supposed to be. Teens with additional struggles can be
completely self-absorbed. They live with the problem
24/7 and are often consumed with it. They may show little
empathy and become defensive and withdrawn. They aren't
talking, at least not to you. And when you try to talk, they
make exasperated faces and pull away even more. So what's
the trick? Patience, perseverance, and genuine curiosity.

A self-absorbed teen doesn't want to hear your story, your
advice, or your experience. She doesn't care that you've been
there and totally understand. She doesn't believe you—and
she's right. You are not her and your life circumstances aren't
the same as hers. You don't really understand. So ask, gently,
consistently, and with curiosity about what she's thinking,
feeling, pondering, confused or even angry about. Then listen
to whatever she's willing to share, whenever she's willing to
share it. Thank her for trusting you and don't tell her what to
do or give her advice. Let her know you trust her judgment
and appreciate that she's confused, angry, apathetic, or sad.

Listening without judgment or advice can be difficult
with a teen who's acting out, and yet she needs that listening
so badly because people are primarily focused on her

behavior. Her feelings are often relegated to "later, when you've changed your behavior."

Can you do that? Can you listen without judgment or advice? Can you listen with empathy and curiosity? Can you put aside your fear and stay curious about your teenager's thinking and problem solving? Can you listen and care, even as you allow your kid to experience the natural consequences of his choices? Listening without judgment is necessary for a slow parenting relationship with your teen. This is a developed skill—you never completely master it, and you'll always be refining your technique.

You also must parent every day because when additional problems or big issues are happening for a teenager, things change not only day to day, but minute to minute. You need to invite her into regular conversation and interaction. Do not give up. You may invite him every day for years, and he might never talk with you about his struggles. But your invitation communicates something beyond words. You're saying, "You matter to me; I want to interact with you no matter your mood or problems. My love and parenting isn't conditional to having you behave a certain way. I love you, and I will not give up on you no matter how you respond or don't respond."

That level of love and acceptance won't fix whatever the problem is, but it *will* pave the road to a more positive relationship with your teenager, now and in the future. It can also help undo any damage that has already been done. You may be coming to Slow Parenting Teens because your relationship with your teenager is non-existent or contentious and difficult. You may wonder if it's too late to have a close, fun relationship due to the many problems your family has had to address. We don't think it's ever too late to improve your relationships. However, we ask you to measure your parenting success in the context of your family situation and your current relationship with your teen.

What are realistic expectations when you start slow parenting after serious problems and mistrust on both sides? You'll notice improvements, and you'll begin to like your teen more when you use the five attitudes. Fights will lessen and arguments will end more quickly. You'll see things earlier and hopefully be able to address issues with less defensiveness on both sides, yours and hers.

The first changes you notice will be lessening of the bad relationship. You'll see less contention and defensiveness, less eye rolling and swearing. And then one day, if you're paying attention, you'll notice your teenager is staying in the room to watch the movie with the rest of the family, lingering at the dinner table just a few minutes longer, saying something nice to a sibling, asking your opinion about a small thing, or even hugging you. The process begins with small, almost unnoticeable behaviors as they test the water to see if you're "walking your talk."

He might wonder if you'll really stop what you're doing and listen to him. Will you truly not punish her if she calls you to pick her up from the party because she's too drunk to drive? Are you genuinely thanking him for cleaning his room, with no corrections or suggestions for how he could do it better? Your teen will be watching and listening to you, even if you don't see it. Your sincerity and perseverance will determine the positive changes in your relationship.

Get support while you move toward slow. We all need it. Even the authors of this book turn to each other when our kids hit a button or our childhood issues get in the way. We often have to ask ourselves, "What are you afraid of?" and then listen as our fears surface. We, too, tend to identify the fears "for our teen" before we can get to the fears for ourselves. No formula works every time with every kid. Your relationship will ebb and flow. Slow Parenting Teens will help you to flow toward a more fun, easy, open relationship with your teen, but please take into account your personal starting place when measuring your success.

Slow parenting teenagers with big problems *does* work to build a more open and connected relationship. Often the damage from the problem means that *relationship repair* needs to be done before *relationship building* can begin. Repairing your relationship is progress. You may think the changes are microscopic, so notice what's working and catch yourself and your teen doing it right. *Slow Parenting Teens* won't fix the problems, but it will help you move through those problems together.

EXERCISE

Answer These Questions to Help Repair and Strengthen Relationships When Your Family Has Big Problems

1. Do you define your teenager/family as troubled? Why?

2. Is your family challenged by some of the problems identified in this chapter? Which ones?

3. How do you currently measure your success as a parent?

4. How do you want your teen to handle feelings and choices?

5. What are you role modeling for your teen regarding your own feelings and choices?

6. Where can you allow more natural consequences instead of setting limits for your teenager?

7. Pick one of the five attitudes and practice it every day for one week. Grade yourself (A, B, or C) each day as you track your progress.

Chapter Fourteen

Resources for Slow Parents

*I*f you're reading this, chances are you're looking for additional references about slow parenting. This chapter will tell you about our favorite books and authors, plus helpful websites and blogs. We encourage you to look on book shelves and search the internet for new material. We hope you'll seek out other parents who are trying to develop slow parenting relationships with their teens. We'll also give you ideas on how to find like-minded folks in your community.

The idea of slow parenting has been around for a few years and was first popularized by Carl Honoré. His book, *Under Pressure: Putting the Child Back into Childhood* (HarperCollins, 2008), used the phrase *slow parenting* and addresses how our current culture creates stress for our children; stress that imitates adult life and isn't good for them. His compelling book addresses time management, extra-curricular activities, and modern culture as they affect young children. We think these same pressures affect teens and make for tension-filled relations between parents and teens. If you're interested in slow parenting for younger children, this is a good place to start. Time magazine called *Under Pressure* the "gospel of the slow parenting movement." Honoré also wrote *In Praise of Slowness* (HarperCollins, 2004) which is not a parenting book per se, but in it he articulates the Slow Philosophy, which encourages us to do everything as well as we can, not as quickly as possible. In it, Honoré talks about the slow food movement.

Wendy Grolnick and Kathy Seal's *Pressured Parents, Stressed-out Kids* (Prometheus Books, 2007) points out the origins and effects of stressful competition in children's lives. These mothers, one a child psychologist and one a parenting journalist, explain how parents unintentionally contribute to their children's "pressure cooker" of competition. They show parents the way out by turning anxiety about their children's success into positive parenting. They provide guidance for parents who struggle with competition anxiety themselves and who want to help their children thrive as they negotiate our culture's pressure.

Lenore Skenazy's *Free Range Kids: How to Raise Safe, Self-Reliant Children (Without Going Nuts with Worry)* (Jossey-Bass, 2009) made a big splash as did Skenazy's April 1, 2008, *New York Post* column about letting her 9-year-old son ride the subway alone. Skenazy's book is a combination of funny stories and well-documented information. She argues that you risk stealing your children's independence and ability to choose if you don't let them explore the world because you're afraid of what might happen. She addresses specific fears such as drowning, choking, strangers, and abductions. We think she provides perspective.

A long-standing and bestselling book on parenting teens is *Parenting Teens with Love and Logic* by Foster Cline, MD and Jim Fay (Piñon Press, 1992, 2006). Cline and Fay take their love and logic parenting ideas and apply them specifically to teens. Their goal is to help parents raise teens who grow up to be responsible adults. They provide many excellent techniques to help parents handle a wide range of situations.

They also take a hard look at how parents cause themselves problems. They coined the phrase *helicopter parents* for those parents who swoop in and take care of their children's mistakes. We particularly appreciate Cline and Fay's sense of humor and emphasis on allowing natural consequences to do the teaching for you.

We also like *Yes, Your Teen is Crazy* by Michael J. Bradley (Harbor Press, 2002) and Bradley's follow-up titles, *Yes, Your Parents are Crazy* (National Book Network, 2004) and *When Things Get Crazy with Your Teen* (McGraw-Hill, 2008). Bradley's thrust is that parents need to understand and accept their teenagers as they are and then *parents* need to change their own behavior. He uses current research in neuroscience and psychology to show how and why parents must adapt to the "new teen." He also provides solutions to many specific issues regarding parenting teens, and he does it quickly and with humor.

The Primal Teen by Barbara Strauch (Anchor Books, 2003) was an eye-opener for us when we first read it. Strauch gives a layperson's overview of recent brain research, explaining that teen's brains are going through changes as rapid and confusing as when they were toddlers. Literally, their brains are growing new neural connections so quickly they can't keep track of them. No wonder they get to the top of the stairs and can't remember why they're there. This book is funny, accessible, and clear about the state of the teenaged brain. This knowledge helps parents empathize with their teens and also develop reasonable expectations.

Just as with Honoré, we see the connections between slow parenting and the slow food movement started by Carlo Petrini in Italy in 1986. The basic premise of the slow food movement is that everyone has the right to the pleasure of good food and a responsibility to protect the heritage of food, tradition, and culture that make this pleasure possible. From that fundamental idea, Petrini's organization has mushroomed all over the globe. The *slow* concept is simple enough to cover a wide range of topics, from local food, to preserving biodiversity, to capturing tradition recipes. This grassroots organization holds conventions and encourages groups and individuals to sign the Slow Food Manifesto. Petrini's *Slow Food Revolution: A New Culture for Dining and Living* (Rizzoli International Publications, 2006) is good reading. While we don't claim that food and teenagers are the same, we do believe parents have the right to the pleasure of a fun, sustainable relationship with their teenagers, and they have a responsibility to steward their children, respect them, and listen to them in order to make this wonderful relationship possible.

The ideas of Slow Parenting Teens developed as we read, talked, lived, and raised our children. The books that follow don't directly speak of parenting, but did influence us as we developed Slow Parenting Teens. They share the notion of starting with the end goal in mind. Slow parents start with the goal of a sustainable and fun relationship.

Steven Covey's *Seven Habits of Highly Effective People* (Free Press, 1989, 2004) is certainly not a parenting book, but Covey encourages habits of mind that are common with slow parenting: reflect on what you do and make particular behavior changes with a specific goal in mind. Covey also has a book for parents called *Seven Habits of Highly Effective Families* (MacMillan, 1997).

Dave Ellis' *Falling Awake* (Breakthrough Enterprises, 2002) emphasizes building relationships through listening well. If you'd like to read more about techniques for listening and letting people just empty out their thoughts, this is the book for you.

The 5 Love Languages (Northfield Publishing, 1992, 1995, 2004) by Gary Chapman provides a framework for understanding what motivates the important people in your life. Understanding your teens' love languages helps you to learn about their personalities and how to adjust to them.

Marti Woodward and Fred Dearborn's *Ten Power Protocols* (Strategic Book Publishing, 2009) outlines a method for creating an organization that communicates clearly and honestly. These same ideas can be used in families with a few modifications.

We would be remiss not to mention the literature of 12-step programs such Alcoholics Anonymous, Al-Anon Family Groups, Narcotics Anonymous, and Overeaters Anonymous. We found inspiration in this rich material, especially with regard to identifying, owning, and handling fears, both noble and selfish. If you're familiar with the ideas of AA, Al Anon, or any other programs that deal with codependency, then you should by all means make a point of using them in your parenting. They complement slow parenting very well.

The internet is a terrific source of information for parenting. Website addresses change and blogs come and go, but here are a few we like and have partnered with:

Radical Parenting with Vanessa Van Patten provides timely, topical information and often from the point of view of teen writers. Her website (www.radicalparenting.com) has depth, sophistication, and doesn't shy away from tough topics. Radical Parenting offers a free newsletter.

Parent eSource (www.parentesource.com) is a global, interactive network for parents of pre-adolescents and teens. Amy Kelly, the CEO and mastermind of Parent eSource, welcomes and shares information on parenting teens and provides a central point for parents to connect to their teen's world.

Slow Parenting Teens, too, has a website (www.slowparentingteens.com), a blog (www.blog.slowparentingteens.com) and a Facebook page (www.facebook.com/SlowParentingTeens). We share stories, ideas, and cool resources. Parents who are slowing down share their stories, too. We welcome you and hope you'll join our virtual community.

We've found that certain keywords give valuable results for slow parenting, and we encourage you to give them a try if you're searching for new ideas on the internet. Pair the word "parenting" with "compassion," "acceptance," "unconditional love," and "slow." Add "blog" to the above list, and you will have plenty to read. When you find something helpful, please share it with us at www.blog. slowparentingteens.com.

Finally, if you enjoy face-to-face conversations, we have some ideas. If you'd like to meet with other parents to talk about parenting teenagers, you probably have community resources available. Check your local library and community bulletin boards for announcements about parenting groups or speaker programs. Often, churches and synagogues host parent groups. Check local newspaper listings and call counseling centers, especially those specializing in children and adolescents. You can suggest slow parenting as a topic of discussion. You could also arrange for Marti Woodward and Molly Wingate to do a presentation on slow parenting for your group.

One way to find like-minded parents is to look around as you take your teenagers to places where kids and their parents hang out: orthodontists' offices, parent teacher conferences, driving school, sporting events, music lessons, martial arts, and so on. When you see relationships you admire between parents and their children, strike up a conversation with the parent to see if you can find a time and place to talk. People who like their kids often love talking about them and how they've built their relationship. You'll notice these parents tend not to complain about their children or roll their eyes when discussing their latest exploits. They also celebrate failures that teach great lessons and admit they don't always know what to do. In fact, a large part of how we got to talking about Slow Parenting Teens was the result of us being like-minded and having kids who constantly ran into each other. We found we could use each other as sounding boards. You can find sounding boards, too.

About the Authors

Marti Woodward has a Master of Science degree in Guidance and Counseling and is a single mom of three teen-aged girls. Marti worked in the field of adolescent addiction and also designed and implemented a family program for at-risk adolescents. She has provided training for executives and supervisors and has facilitated workshops for a variety of organizations. As a coach, Marti continues to specialize in adolescent and family issues.

Molly Wingate brings her practice as a parent and educator to Slow Parenting Teens. She co-parents her two, teen-aged sons with her husband, Brian Murphy. They have a two-career, two-station wagon, traditional, nuclear family. She taught high school and college students (teenagers) for over twenty years before starting a writing consulting business. Molly has a B.A. and M.A. in English literature.

CPSIA information can be obtained
at www.ICGtesting.com
Printed in the USA
LVOW01s2223240616

494062LV00016B/79/P